BEN LOGAN

Christmas Remembered

NORTHWORD PRESS
Minnetonka, Minnesota

NorthWord Press
5900 Green Oak Drive
Minnetonka, MN 55343
1-800-328-3895

Cover Images ©1997 PhotoDisc / ©1997 Corel Corporation
Book design by Russell S. Kuepper
Illustrations by Amy Quamme

Library of Congress Cataloging-in-Publication Data

Logan, Ben
    Christmas remembered / by Ben Logan.
       p. cm.
    ISBN 1-55971-636-3 (hardcover)
    1. Christmas--Wisconsin. 2. Wisconsin--Social life and customs.
  I. Title.
  GT4986.W6L64 1997   97-9616
  394.2663'09775--dc21   CIP

Printed in U.S.A.

Table of Contents

Looking for Christmas

I woke to a howling around the eaves, that weather-voice telling me of bare trees which no longer tempered the winds. The voice spoke of winter. I had not yet said good-bye to summer.

Time, using an energy of its own, shifts easily back and forth across the years in my house. There in the bedroom where I was born, I reached up and touched axe-hewn logs that have been in place more than a hundred years, my hands trying to link the then and the now of myself.

I live in the house alone, having come back after a half-century to the Wisconsin farm where I grew up. Friends in the East worried about me when I tore up roots there, afraid I was trying to go backward in time. I told them it was all right, that I could go home again—just so I didn't try to be the same person I was when I left.

I had spoken too easily. With the wind trying to make me part of winter before I was ready, I felt immobilized, unclaimed by past or present or any season.

Christmas was part of the problem. My daughter Kristine had called the evening before, asking me what I wanted this year. I looked at the great jumble of unanswered letters and unfinished manuscripts on my desk and said, "Why are you talking about Christmas when I am only halfway through July?"

"It's only four weeks away," she said.

I had gone to sleep thinking about Christmas, feeling no connection with a season that had been so important to me in the past. That was how I was thinking of it—in the past—important for children, an idea that adults cling to as a way of clinging to childhood. I had never before asked myself, "What is Christmas?" It had been too real to need definition. Now I had either deserted Christmas or it had deserted me.

When I got out of bed and built the fires, the sense of having lost Christmas dominated my day, following me from room to room of the old farmhouse. In early afternoon I walked out across the fields to my favorite thinking place, wondering how one searches for a lost Christmas. I laughed when I found myself asking, "Can the me of now, living on land filled with echoes, look for the meaning of past Christmases and the me of then without getting the two of us mixed up?"

My thinking place is the same hilltop where I sat as a child and pondered the unanswerable questions of life. Three old and wonderfully gnarled bur oaks partially hid the narrow hollow below, their branches swaying, cracking against each other. Fallen leaves, refusing to be motionless and let summer and autumn die, blew with a dry skittering sound along the hillside. A single milkweed down, seed already dropped to earth somewhere, sailed past my face, then soared up through the trees and out of sight. Behind me, a bittersweet vine crawled along the wires of the fence, berries bright red, open hulls bright yellow. A wind-blown crow flew crookedly above the meadow.

I watched and listened, realizing how often I do that—one by one finding the components of a day and fitting them together into a wholeness that reconnects me with the beauty and mystery of the land.

Could I do the same for Christmas?

A cherry "*chick-a-dee-dee*" brought my eyes back toward the hillside. The chickadee hung half upside down on a swaying twig, looking at me (inquisitively, I swear) as though asking if I would like some company.

I smiled at the bird. I always do when one joins me. There is some marvelous, warming delight in those bits of flesh and feathers, so sprightly and audacious, so tiny and vulnerable, so goodhearted and courageous.

CHAPTER ONE

"So, what is Christmas?" I asked.

The chickadee did not answer.

I started a fire in the circle of stones on the hillside, then sat on a log close to that warmth and tried to find my way back to the earliest Christmases I could remember. At first it was all questions. How could those Christmases have been such a part of me, yet seem to come from outside me? How could they have been so new each year, yet always be the same Christmas, the way it is with an old and familiar tree that is always there but always has new growth.

Memory does not like to be forced into a neat chronology. I was assaulted by random fragments—a color, a smell, a voice in song, a happy face, the jingle of sleigh bells, neighbors coming across the field, lighting their way with a lantern.

I pounced on each fragment, trying to hold and enlarge it, succeeding only for a moment before it flitted away from me, the way it is with a dream when I first wake up.

I sat for a long time, until the rising wind and afternoon cold drove me back across the fields to the house. I put fresh wood on the embered fire. Then I went to my typewriter. There, I have learned, I can let the fragments of memory flow out through the ends of my fingers and take form on paper. It is when I read those words that I discover where I have been and what my years have taught me.

That is how this search began. I found Christmas, of course. I found missing pieces of myself. All of it was different than I expected because I began remembering much that I did not know I had stored so carefully inside me.

Christmas Kalidescope

I was hillborn, brought into life in southwestern Wisconsin's rough and beautiful land. There I learned as a child, without knowing I was learning, that the year has five seasons, not four.

Christmas was the fifth season. It reached out to us on our ridge-top farm, interrupting those tag end days of the year when wind howled around eaves, and our spirits were as shriveled as the few stubborn apples still clinging to the Wolf River tree. In years of depression or plenty, happy times or sad times, land sparkling with white or laying bare and gray, the season of Christmas found us, bringing so much, seeming to ask so little in return. Each year I longed for its coming, then joined it and did not want it ever to end.

Even when I was very young, Christmas was already a time of memory. It reached back beyond my birth. I could see earlier Christmases in the way Mother hung a favorite, faded ornament on the tree, the way Father's face softened when he sang a Christmas carol in Norwegian, and in stories told by my three older brothers.

Reach back into all the Christmases of these early years and what do I find? It is all bits and pieces, everything one at a time. I am looking again into my first kaleidoscope, A Christmas present identical to that of my brother, Lee, but I could not and do not believe his had images half as fabulous as mine.

A kaleidoscope, of course, is an instrument of magic. Shake it! Look into it! Random fragments move into patterns, some just color and beauty, others subtle beginnings of something almost familiar. Then the mind, which is also an instrument of magic, can seize those beginnings, make them grow and connect them into a whole, the way one can assemble the pieces of a puzzle.

Shake the kaleidoscope of memory, close my eyes and it begins to happen. Only then, going back beyond thought, beyond too neatly arranged chronologies of time and taken-for-granted rituals that hide the truth, do I find glimpses of what made it Christmas.

Shake the kaleidoscope. I am scratching through frost on my bedroom window to find if the outside world looks different on Christmas morning. I find a lifeless-looking stillness, the white curve of a hilltop field like the outline of a sleeping miniature planet, and beyond it the woods where brown leaves cling to the white oaks. It is all silent and frozen, and summer will never come again. As though to argue with me and say the land is never still and lifeless, there is movement. A rust brown color that seems bright as a summer flower is moving along the curve of the hilltop field—a red fox, almost strutting as though it knows I am watching.

Close my eyes again. I am in the cellar, surrounded by smells from the earth, the orange light of my lantern barely holding back the watching, cobwebbed darkness. Whistling bravely, I snatch potatoes from the big bin, dig beets and carrots from boxes of sand, grab jars of fruits and vegetables from the shelves. Making several trips up the steep stairs, escaping the pursuing darkness just in time, I pile my treasures on the pantry floor and slam shut the trap door. Mother, seeing that, gives me a hug, and smiles at the gathered bounty, her mind already putting it together into Christmas dinner.

Shake the kaleidoscope. A bright red cardinal is on a bough of the white pine beyond the porch, new-fallen snow on the green behind it. It sits as though waiting to be noticed, because this is Christmas Day and it can decorate a tree as well as we can. I move closer. The cardinal flits away, bringing down a flurry of white flakes that glitter and change color, red and blue and yellow, as they fall through the sunlight.

Then it is a bleak, soggy day and we are taking the tobacco down from the shed, even if it is Christmas, handing the fog-softened plants, that are speared onto laths, to someone below, who hands them to someone farther below, who piles them. Chilled to the bone, we go back to a house filled with cooking smells and we huddle around the stove. Pinpoints of orange flame and tiny puffs of smoke escape where sheets of black metal join, the burning wood giving us the closest thing to sun we have seen for days.

Shake the kaleidoscope. One of my brothers is saying, as one of them will say every year, "Remember the time the dog knocked the Christmas tree down?" Had they thought about it, surely my brothers would have said that I was too small then to "know anything about anything." That does not matter. The kaleidoscope tells me I am part of the story. I can see a brown and white dog peering out from beneath the tree, a string of white popcorn in his mouth. I can see the dog being untangled from the strings. I can see my mother rescuing an ornament, cradling it a moment in her hands. I can hear the laughter and almost surely there is discussion (called arguing when parents are present) about who cut the crossboards at the bottom of the tree too short, or would it have happened anyway because someone mixed up the bowls and put already-buttered popcorn on the string? Then, the tree is straight again and Mother lights the candles, first putting the dog outside, of course, and Father, never trusting the combination of pine needles and candle flames, stands by with a bucket of water.

Shake the kaleidoscope again. My brothers and I are hurtling down the hillside on our sleds, coasting on past the steaming, open water of the spring, all the way to the creek. Two neighbor boys join us and we take long runs along the creek bank, then step onto the ice and slide as far as we can go, teetering and yelling, trying not to fall and almost always falling.

Our legs tangled up with one another, and too weak from laughing to get up, we sprawl with out heads on the ice, hearing the creek water bubbling its way downstream to the rivers and to the sea. And we argue about whether or not the creek water will ever return as rain.

"But how would you know it's the same water?"

"How long does it take?"

"Why isn't it salty, if it comes back from the sea?" That would be the voice of my skeptical brother, Junior.

Voices still linking us in the dusk, the four of us and the two neighbor boys climb our separate hillsides toward home, sleds rattling behind us weighing a thousand pounds, and we go on yelling back and forth until there is nothing left but echoes. Then we are back in the warm house, starving and eating Christmas dinner all over again.

Look back again. I am in the Lewis Store in Gays Mills. Father searches for a Christmas present for Mother, seeming awkward in that section of the store where all the other shoppers are women. He holds up a rose-colored comforter and looks at me and asks "What do you think?"

"It's beautiful," I say, and his face has the broadest smile I have ever seen there. At home I clutch the comforter close to me, feeling its warmth, as I steal silently into the house while Father distracts Mother in the kitchen. I force the resisting bulk into a cardboard box and hide it under my bed, knowing I will have to watch carefully and move it at least once before Christmas. Mother is a determined sweeper and enemy of winter dust. Finally, it is Christmas morning. She holds the comforter against her, tears in her eyes, cheeks matching the rose of the cloth, and she goes to Father and gives him a hug.

Memory of the comforter does not end there. It became a special part of our lives, its color and warmth covering each of us in turn when we were ill and slept on the dining room couch. There, close to the heating stove and the open door to Father and Mother's bedroom, I can feel the comforter being pulled up close to my face as Mother "tucks me in," then blows out the kerosene lamp, the charring wick leaving a momentary glow in the room.

Shake the kaleidoscope. I see the orange, winking light of kerosene lanterns moving across the fields in early evening darkness, and soon the house is warmed with neighbors. There is play, laughter and music, the smell of popcorn, cocoa and coffee. Then something in Christmas brings back the old tales, my own father sailing from Norway in 1898, new settlers coming in, others moving on to places greener, freer, emptier or whatever it is that always lies to the West.

A neighbor man, the one with a mournful face, says something about "the lost frontier." Then, there is talk about what is gone—passenger pigeons, bears, elk, wolves, the Indians, land virgin and unspoiled, streams running clear after rains. There is even a dim, passed-on from earlier generations memory of buffalo. Another man says he read somewhere that the last one in Wisconsin was killed in 1832.

The man with the mournful face says, "Lot of things we could have done better."

There is a silence after the man's words. I can feel a sadness in the room. I expect it to be Mother who will find a way to rescue Christmas from this sudden somberness. But it is Father. He sits nodding, staring straight ahead. He did that sometimes in the middle of a conversation. I always thought he was arranging his Norwegian thoughts into his careful English. "Well," he says. "I think the question is not did we always do the best we could have. The question is do we learn anything as we go along, then do better next time."

Mother pours more coffee and cocoa. The talk goes back to lighter things, stories that begin with "Remember the time . . ." and bring us back to laughter and the familiar feel of Christmas.

Then the winking lanterns take the neighbors back across the snow-covered fields to home, the voices and the pungent smell of corncob pipe smoke still floating through the house.

The years, looked at through the kaleidoscope, are not neatly organized. It is not time, but ideas and feelings, that link us together and give continuity to our lives.

Suddenly it is another Christmas season, one without snow, and I am with Father. The two of us walk out across one of the fields. He is telling me about his childhood in Norway and I can see him running with his brothers along a path that is close to the cold North Sea. His face is open and smiling, his sternness put aside for Christmas along with worries about a new growing season that may be filled with drought or insects or hail or weather too hot for oats and too cold for corn. The northwest wind tears at our coats. In the plowed field under out feet, puffs of soil are picked up and are drifting off like black snow. Father sees that happening and frowns. I can almost hear him thinking, "It took a hundred years to make an inch of that topsoil." I hold my breath, afraid I will lose him too soon back into the non-Christmas world. "Have to do that different another year," is all he says. He smiles and puts his hand on my shoulder. We turn and walk, side by side like two adults, into the cutting wind, back toward the farmhouse, smoke from the chimneys telling us of the warmth that waits for us there.

Go on shaking the kaleidoscope and the images come faster and faster. Strings of red cranberries on the tree. Sundogs in the west. A snowy owl sitting in the oak we call the section tree. Father quietly singing a Norwegian song as he reads for the third, fourth, or fifth time a letter from his mother. The incredible red of a Delicious apple. The ripping sound of a Hubbard squash opening ahead of the knife. Bread dough, filled with living yeast, rising above the sides of the bowl. Bittersweet berries encased in ice. Tea kettle lifting its lid up and down, sending puffs of steam out the spout. A pan of hot fudge melting a hole down into crusted snow. Steam from the body heat of the cattle coming out around the edge of the barn door, and the stored smell of summer in the haymow. A single red leaf, driven from hiding by wind, blowing along the top of the snow. A tinseled star at the top of the tree, always speaking of ancient times and three wise men, reminding me of Father as a young sailor on the open sea, guided home by stars, lighthouses, and, now, by Mother's lamp in the kitchen window.

They are unending, those bits and pieces of childhood years, so close to me I can almost reach out and touch the heart of Christmas, so full of people I have loved, so linked with knowing I am part of the living land, so filled with who and what I am.

I let the images come again.

I am seeing Mother at the zinc-topped kitchen table planning our Christmas, bringing all of herself back from whatever dreams sometimes took her off alone in her mind to other places, finding in this fifth season of the year whatever it was she searched for.

I see myself and my brothers, some of our bickering stilled at Christmas, playing together, needing each other, taste buds of the mind all turned on, and we are filled with a sense of newness and belonging that carries us on past Three Kings' Days into the faithful seasons of another year.

The Year
the Presents
Didn't Come

I have been a wanderer. I seem to have some special talent for taking the past along with me into the
present, making a home of wherever I find myself.
Yet, over the years the word Christmas has trans-
ported me from anywhere on Earth back to the farm
we called "Seldom Seen." The Christmases of my
childhood on this high ridge merge now into one continuing memory.

Some years, though, come back more clearly, different enough to earn names for themselves—the year there wasn't any snow, the year we didn't have a Christmas tree, the year we got the pony, the year the dog knocked over the tree.

There was another special year, when I was very young and Christmas was still more things than spirit to me. The remembered happy and sad feelings, and the events, smells and colors of that Christmas became "the year the presents didn't come."

The first promise of Christmas announced itself on a day when brown grass of late summer crackled under our bare feet as we raced to meet the mailman and were handed the first of the Fall/Winter mail-order catalogs. George Holliday smiled and said, as he always did each time he delivered a catalog, "Here's the new 'want book,' boys. Merry Christmas!"

Once, George Holliday's old Model T Ford came groaning up to the mailbox, rear end sagging, steam shooting up from the boiling radiator. "Hell's Bells!" he yelled. "Come and get some of these cussed things out of here before my springs give out!"

The whole back of the Model T was piled with catalogs. It was a miracle! All the different ones had come on the same day—Montgomery Ward, Sears-Roebuck, and Savage.

"A pity there isn't one more company," Mother said. "Then there would be enough to go around."

I don't think that would have helped. Each catalog had its specialties, each a separate doorway to a world we could only dream about there on our hilltop farm. The four of us would sprawl on the lawn under the big maple tree, grabbing, fighting, arguing over what to look at first. Laurance, the oldest, wanted to see the rifles. Junior was torn between auto parts and guitars. Lee demanded the saddles and carbide lamps for exploring non-existent caves. I, the youngest, could not see any sense wasting time on all that when the toys were still waiting to be discovered.

When it was time to go back to the blazing sun of the hay fields, we would start fighting all over again about who had dibs for which catalog after the chores were done that evening. Then, gathered at the dining room table in the yellow light of the Rayo kerosene lamp, the battle went on. If our parents ever got a look into a newly arrived catalog it must have been after we had gone to bed, though sometimes the catalogs went with us and Father never knew why the flashlight batteries went dead so fast.

Once Mother announced it was her turn. We took the catalogs to her at the end of the table nearest the kitchen. Before she got past the cover of the first one we were crowded behind her chair peering over her shoulder, already arguing and pushing. She sent us off to bed and I never knew what she turned to look at first. Was it adult things or childhood things?

Those catalogs, it must be understood, were our department stores. Visitors from a marvelous place somewhere outside our world, they said Christmas was coming, that once a year a spirit of extravagance brought us a select few of all the wonderful things on display.

Because we memorized in minute detail every item of importance, there was no way for Christmas presents to be a complete surprise. If a thing existed, it was in the catalogs and we had seen it. Finally, Mother and Father gave up trying to guess just right. On a year before I can remember, a change was made. We were allowed a certain amount of money and could pick out our own presents from the catalogs.

That may have simplified it all for Father and Mother. It did not simplify it for me. A day would come in November when it was my turn to sit down with Mother at the dining room table, catalogs spread around us, to make my impossible choices. But how could I do that when each year all those dozens and dozens of toys could wind themselves up and run right off the pages into my waiting mind?

There were trucks and cars with growling motors, and a miniature filling station and a gas pump with a ringing bell for each gallon. A wobbling, shaking "Limping Lizzie" automobile had a sign that said "Four Wheels—No Brakes" but I didn't need that because I had the mailman's falling-apart Model T Ford to laugh at. There was a rabbit that jumped when you squeezed a rubber bulb, a trick glass that dribbled, and a squawker to put on someone's chair—never a parent's chair and almost never a teacher's.

A tight-strung bow set included an arrow with a rubber suction cup to be used for frightening adults by sticking the arrow onto the middle of your forehead. Tin pistols that fired "5,000 sparking flashes before reloading" and long before that were left on the floor and stepped on. A drum with a genuine leather head, to be pounded loudly until an elder brother asked if I knew what was hidden inside the drum and offered to loan me his pocket knife.

Airplanes with propellers that whirled when held up to the wind, a fire truck with crank-up ladders for rescuing screaming children from burning buildings and cats from tall trees, and another truck with a little lever for dumping sand or dust out in the yard—and once, for a wonderful, glistening white moment, a full pound of sugar on Mother's bright red living-room rug.

There were unnecessary things, called "Playthings that instruct"—educational games, blackboards and carpentry sets with safe, toothless saws. A separate section for girls—dolls, cribs, miniature kitchen ranges, ironing boards, brooms and dustpans, and once, offending all logic, a four-wheeled "tricycle" that would not tip over. Sisterless, as I was, I wondered if girls were ever supposed to have any fun at all.

There were cruel and impossibly out-of-reach things that rich city cousins might someday own—bicycles, electric trains, pedal cars and "fully functional" steam engines with tiny boilers that promised the possibility of explosions.

There were erector sets with a million little nuts and bolts that got lost on the floor, and Lyle, the hired man, jumped and swore when he stepped on them in his stocking fee. Cap pistols came without ammunition (not shippable by mail) but we children knew that the carefully cut-off tips of forbidden wooden matches would make a "CRACK!" and a most satisfactory puff of white smoke and sulfur smell.

There were Tinkertoys and blocks for creating buildings and previously uninvented machines that were laughed at and knocked down by older brothers. And a wind-up World War I tank with rubber treads that always came off when pounced on by the almost surely German cat. And a little music box with a yellow knob to be cranked and cranked until the only sound left was a nerve-jangling clicking and no one understood that I went on cranking anyway because I could still hear the fragment of song playing inside my head.

Finally, when I was totally lost among the remembered toys of other Christmases and the seemingly unending offerings of current catalogs, my patient mother would try to rescue me. "You keep turning back to look at the blue truck. Is that what you want? And if it is, what else do you want for the thirty-one cents you have left?"

"A top, maybe!" A whistling top with bright-colored stars that would turn into stripes when it whirled and hummed a deep-throated sound like something from another planet.

"That top is more than thirty-one cents. Wouldn't this other one do?"

"No. No. No. The colors are different. Maybe the car with red wheels, instead."

"This one?"

"No. No. No. Red wheels with white sidewalls and a crank sticking out in front."

"Are you sure? Won't a truck and a car be too much alike?"

"I'm sure." Grownups were strange back then. How was it possible to think that a car with red wheels and white sidewalls was at all like a blue truck?

Mother would sigh and write it down on the order form. She was our keeper of the rituals of special days and was uneasy with all this picking and choosing and counting up the money. "Doesn't it spoil it for you, having seen what you are going to get?" she would ask. We would tell her no, but we knew it bothered her. How can a child tell a grownup that a picture is only a picture and that when the real toy comes free of the wrapping paper and is held in the hands, it is new and has never been seen before?

The catalog orders would go into the mail and our choices began to grow, becoming our own creations. Every morning when I first woke up, I would stay under the covers a moment, shut my eyes tight and try to see what was happening. After five days I decided the letter had arrived in Chicago. Two more days— no, make it three because they were busy—to find our things and ship them. Then another five days for the packages to come. I added one more day because that made it Saturday and I could run to meet the mailman myself. Mr. Holliday was driving a sled by then because there was too much snow for his Model T. He poked through the packages in the sled box. "Sorry," he said. "Not here yet."

He listened carefully when I told him about the schedule I had allowed. "I figure about another six days," he said.

"Make it seven," I said.

"Why?"

"It'll be Saturday again."

"Seven days it is," he said, "since that's important."

It was important all right. If I could get a package myself and walk slowly to the house, I could squeeze it a little and maybe identify things. Sometimes there might be a little tear in the brown wrapping paper and maybe a flash of color from inside if I turned the package just right. I almost never made the holes larger.

At the one room school in Halls Branch Valley, Teacher asked, as she always did the last week before vacation, "What do you want for Christmas this year?"

We recited our hopes and choices—dolls, sleds, teddy bears, skis, ball gloves, BB guns. One boy always requested a pet skunk. And, of course, a big blue truck and a car with red wheels and whitewall tires.

Just the listing of them made the things more real, the waiting more agonizing. Teacher kept trying to get our attention, making us practice our lines and songs for the annual Christmas program. She couldn't seem to understand that our minds belonged to Christmas now, not to her.

Saturday came. I ran halfway out to Denny Meagher's woods to meet the mailman. He leaned down and handed me some letters and a magazine. "No packages today. I guess we need to give it 'til next week."

The days crept by. School was out and each forenoon we waited in the cold for Mr. Holliday. He would search through the sled for the packages he already knew were not there and say, "Maybe tomorrow."

We would run to tell Father and Mother, watching their faces for clues of what they were going to do about it. They didn't ask questions about substitute presents. There were no shopping trips to see what might be found at the country stores in Seneca, Petersburg and Gays Mills.

The four of us would go outside again and talk about it. Maybe there wasn't enough money to buy things at the stores after writing the checks to the mail-order companies. Maybe they had other reasons.

On the day before Christmas we raced to the mailbox with a half-gallon pail of steaming coffee for Mr. Holliday. "You know," he said, not looking at us, "I guess nothing came, but I'll just look one more time." His voice was gruff. He sorted through the packages. We knew there wasn't anything there for us. He was just trying to make us feel better, or maybe make himself feel better.

He turned to us and rubbed his mitten across his chin. "I'm sorry. I hear tell there's been a big train wreck down toward Chicago. Lot of things not coming through. Tell you what, I'll telephone if anything comes in on the afternoon train."

He took the bucket of coffee and drove on.

We stayed there at the mailbox looking at each other. We didn't believe it. Was there any chance Mother was playing a trick on us? Once she had caught me investigating the packages in the dark closet under the stairway. "Won't be the same for you now on Christmas day, will it?" was all she said. From then on she hid the presents better. But she wouldn't let us think no presents had come, would she? We stood kicking at the snow to keep our feet warm and we talked about the train wreck. I could imagine our presents scattered in the snow and a mean-looking boy playing with my blue truck, pushing down too hard, bending a wheel, scraping a freshly painted fender against a rock.

I was crying when we went to the house.

Mother held me. "We'll still have Christmas, you know."

"Without our presents?"

Something changed in her face. "There's more to Christmas than presents."

The day turned colder in midafternoon. Snow began to fall from the colorless sky. Time for the afternoon train passed. There was no telephone call.

Mother had to remind us to get the tree. That meant choosing two or three boughs from one of the tall white pines in the yard and lashing them together to look like a regular tree. The four of us did that, our jackets turning white. There was none of our usual arguments about which boughs, how long should they be and did the tree have to look perfect even on the side that would be turned to the wall.

When we carried the tree in and set it up in the dining room, the fresh snow began to melt into hundreds of shiny beads of water.

"Look!" Mother said. "It's already decorated."

We popped corn and made strings, the white corn alternating with red cranberries. We got out all the old ornaments, handing to Father the star that went at the very top and the others that went up high, beyond our reach. The folded paper ornaments were opened to become bright colored balls, stars and bells. Mother began to hum a Christmas carol. The cat played with the strings of popcorn and berries, was chased away, then came sneaking back to pounce and be chased away again. It was just like all the other remembered afternoons leading up to Christmas Eve, but soon I sat down behind the heating stove and just watched.

The house was very still when I woke on Christmas morning. There was ice on the covers from my breathing. Treelike patterns of frost covered the lower half of my window, turned red-gold by the beginning color on the eastern horizon. Far out across a white meadow I could see smoke rising from the chimney of a neighbor's house, reminding me that other people were having Christmas.

I heard Father get up and rekindle the fires. The smell of woodsmoke filled the house. The dining room was already warm when I went down to breakfast, candle flames flickering on the tree and Father standing by with a bucket of water "just in case." Mother had put a great bunch of bittersweet in the middle of the table, the yellow hulls open, showing the bright red berries.

For each of us there was a basket filled with English walnuts, pecans, almonds, ribbon candy, peanut brittle, chocolate stars, and one bright navel orange and a big red Delicious apple. Already my brothers were making deals about sharing halves of apples and oranges because they were too special to be eaten all at once.

I sorted through my basket, silenced by the strangeness of having no presents to open and the thought of an empty day stretching ahead.

After the outdoor chores were done, we gathered again in the warm dining room and Father and Mother took turns reading aloud the Christmas letters from people far away. One letter, in an envelope lined with bright colored paper, was from Father's mother, the grandmother I had never seen. Father read slowly, translating the Norwegian words.

Someone interrupted with a question about his mother and he got out old pictures of her for us to see. He finished the letter and we began asking other questions. He answered, staring off into space sometimes as though he could look back to Norway and find exactly the right details to use in describing something from his childhood.

I didn't remember Father ever talking to us that way before. I kept looking at the pictures from Norway, wondering about him. I had never thought of my father as once being as young as I and all excited about Christmas.

When the letters were finished and the arguing about who got which stamps was over, Mother went to the kitchen to work on Christmas dinner. We four boys followed and worked with her. I don't think that had ever happened before. My new toys had always captured me on Christmas morning, pulling me away into a play world that did not include anyone else.

We made sugar cookies, eating them hot and buttery right from the oven almost as fast as we cut out new ones. The chickens were already cooking, filling the house with a rich roasting smell. Junior brought his guitar into the kitchen and we sang as we worked. Not Christmas carols. They were for later. Everyone kept talking about earlier Christmases, every other sentence beginning with "Remember the time . . . ."

Mother helped me into the cellar, down through the creaking trap door in the pantry floor, and handed me a kerosene lantern. I picked out especially good potatoes from the big bin, dug carrots from the boxes of sand, chose a Hubbard squash, found jars of pickled crab apples and fished slippery dill pickles from the ten-gallon crock.

Cranberries were bubbling on the stove when I came back to the kitchen. "Why do some of them float?" I asked, reminding Mother of how I tested "questionable" eggs. The bad ones floated in a bucket of water.

Mother laughed. "I don't know why some cranberries float, but they are all good."

She handed me a wooden spoon and let me pop the floating berries against the side of the pan. She winked at me. "My cook book says not to do that. But my mother let me do it and now you're doing it."

While Mother made the pies—pumpkin, apple and mincemeat, we tried to make popcorn balls. The caramel made them so sticky we could only get them out of our hands by eating them right then.

Everyone was busy every minute. There were hickory nuts to crack, bowls to lick, coffee to grind, cream to whip. We kept splitting more fine wood and feeding the kitchen range to keep the fire just right.

Finally, we all helped carry the steaming dishes to the dining room table with its white tablecloth that was trimmed with lace. There was a solemn moment and then the food itself, delicious and unending.

After dinner, Father left the table and put on his heavy jacket. We knew what he was going to do. Every year he took down a sheaf of oats that had been hanging on the wall since harvest and carried it outside for the birds.

This time we put on our coats and went with him.

"It was something we did in Norway," he told us. "But there it would be always wheat."

He hung the oats on the big maple tree and we stepped back and waited, standing very still. A blue jay swooped in and peered at the grain. A bright red cardinal came and began to eat. Then a whole flock of English sparrows arrived, noisy and quarrelsome, reminding me of the four of us.

Father turned to look out over the snow-covered fields. He was smiling and nodding his head. "You know," he said, sounding surprised, "I had almost forgotten. We always had a big bonfire at Christmas, too."

"Why a bonfire?" I asked.

He laughed and put a hand on my shoulder. "Why I think there was a kind of legend about it. Days kept getting shorter that time of the year. Even shorter in Norway than here. The sun seemed to be tired, like it almost couldn't get above the horizon anymore. So, at Christmas we built bonfires to help warm up the sun, bring the sun back to life for another year."

"Could we do that?" I asked. "Have a bonfire?"

"Yes," he said. "Let us do that."

We cleared the snow away, brought kindling and sticks of oak from the woodshed and soon had a roaring bonfire going in the yard. I ran to tell Mother and she put on her coat and joined us. The flames climbed up into the gray sky. Sparks sailed high above the yard.

We stood in a circle around the fire, jackets unbuttoned in the heat. Father linked his hand with Mother's and began singing a song in Norwegian. We tried to join him, stumbling over the strange words.

I kept looking up at the sky, expecting the sun to shine.

When the fire had burned down to embers, we went back inside. We put more wood in the stoves and Mother played the piano for carol singing. I stood close beside her, singing with everyone else. Between songs, Mother smiled at me, gave me a hug and said, "Merry Christmas!"

Even then I don't think I realized how different the day had been. That is the way of Christmas stories. Their meanings have to grow with the seasons and the telling, and we only remember what we have learned by keeping the past alive.

A year later, Teacher asked as always, what we wanted for Christmas. One by one the answers came—a doll, a BB gun, a sled, a pet skunk. Then it was my turn. I knew what I had asked for—a bright red fire engine. I almost said that.

Teacher waited, then smiled and said, "Not sure yet?"

I nodded and let it go at that, unwilling to speak with all those faces watching and waiting, not quite sure how to say, "I just want it to be Christmas."

Christmas Cookies

One of my tasks on the day before Christmas was taking cookies to the neighbors. I did it by myself, perhaps wanting to get away sometimes from my three brothers who were always part parent to me. I am tempted to say I was the cookie deliverer every year, but I find that memory is very selective. It seeks the unusual and can trick me.

So perhaps it was not every year that I delivered the cookies, because I mostly seem to be remembering a year when I tugged along my new sled, with the bright red eagle painted on it, as I trekked out to the scattered farmhouses.

I went first along the ridge to the east where Mrs. Pete Zintz, bent down with arthritis, hugged me to her flour sack apron. Her husband had died and she lived there with a bachelor son who always went off somewhere at Christmas.

Mrs. Zintz took me inside. It was dark, green shades pulled down at the windows. She gave me a single cookie that was half the size of a dinner plate and almost equally hard. A sprinkle of red sugar coated the cookie. There was no other feel of Christmas in that house.

I went through the woods to the Oppriecht's. The youngest boy, Claire, had built a snow fort. We hid inside the walls, guarding the cookies, and hurled chunks of crusted snow at enemies who had disguised themselves as tree trunks and clothesline posts.

Enemies conquered, we rewarded ourselves with one cookie each, then went inside to deliver the rest. Claire's grandmother, Mrs. Mulligan, heard us and said, "Who's that who came in with Claire?" I went to her. She ran her age-crooked fingers over my face. "Is it Lee? No, you're Ben. You're the youngest."

Mrs. Mulligan was almost blind. One of my jobs was to run the half-mile across the fields with things for her to do with her hands—peas to shell or string beans to snap in summer, ground cherries to husk in fall.

I left that house, with its feel of Christmas. Still tugging my sled, I broke a trail through the snow to our own land, and headed down into the valley. I followed the frozen-over creek, the sound of water coming through the ice, and went on up the valley to the Watson's.

Bryce, who was my age, was outside in the yard. We ran up the crooked creek valley to look at the deep crevice we called "the Cave." The opening led back into a sandstone cliff. We kept thinking we would find tracks in the snow, because we liked to believe some-one or something must surely live there.

There were no tracks. We listened for sounds from inside. We told ourselves again that, come spring, we would bring shovels and dig at the cave entrance to find the charcoal of old campfires, arrowheads, or maybe even old gold coins buried there in the 1600s by a lost French explorer.

There either was, or we imagined there was, a noise from inside the cave. We raced back down the valley. I gave the cookies to Mrs. Watson, a big woman with a big smile, and she handed me one of her own "to eat on your way back to the ridge."

Sled bouncing behind me, I ran up the narrow hollow to the south for my last delivery. Out of sight from the Watsons and beyond Bryce's voice calling that he would watch the cave for me, I stopped run-ning. I did not want to go up the ridge to that last house.

To my left, a trail led into a side hollow, one of those heavily wooded, narrow places where the sun never seemed to shine. I went that way to see the spring that trickled out of the face of a low cliff. Ice clung to the ledges. Water spilled over the ice, col-lected at the base of the cliff, then ran in a little stream down past the knobbed and twisted red elm tree that was always like a picture from one of my storybooks.

Beyond the tree, sticking up about two feet, was the stone foundation of what long ago might have been a small building or perhaps a well. I brushed snow away and sat perfectly still on the wall, listen-ing and watching as I often did there, for some hint of who had been in that place long before.

Then, something small and black was moving on the snow in front of me. The bit of black, no larger than my finger, stopped. There was a movement ahead of the black. A face appeared, tiny and quick. It was a weasel, the first I had ever seen, all white except for the tip of the tail. It moved again, the face vanishing, the spot of black traveling away from me. I could picture a hawk or an owl swooping down, expecting a mouse and finding nothing but that tip of tail.

A gust of wind came into the hollow. Tree limbs rattled. I looked up and was surprised to see that the buds on silver maples and aspens were already swelling, getting ready for spring, even in the dead of winter.

Blue jays were scolding up on the hillside. There was the bright green of watercress under the ice at the base of the cliff. Old leaves still clung to a white oak tree. Some of them, maybe forced loose by the growing buds, sailed off in the wind to some destination of their own. The leaves were like the water of the spring that ran down to the creek, to the Kickapoo River, to the Wisconsin River, to the Mississippi and, finally, to the Gulf of Mexico.

Something happened to me in that place. I kept looking around at the complexity of it, some part of me wanting to gather all the bits and pieces so I could see what they meant. There was a "presence" in the woods. It reached out to me, asking me to understand a mystery that retreated ahead of my thoughts. I could no more follow it than I could in summer follow the whispering, directionless song of the grasshopper sparrow.

I don't remember how, or how often, I thought of that experience in the days that followed. I do know that I vividly remembered it years later when a college professor, Aldo Leopold, spoke of all things being interconnected and that nothing can be picked up one at a time. He spoke of land in a way new to me. By land, he said, is meant all things on, over or in the earth.

Did it have some special meaning, the fact that this happened to me at Christmas? I like to think so, because "land," as Aldo Leopold spoke of it, is a gift. We are part of it. Land is the gift of life itself.

On that long-ago day, I got up from the old stone foundation, knowing what I had to do. I went back to the larger hollow. I followed it up toward the ridge, to a house whose loneliness would cling to me and follow me away.

There were three people in that farmhouse, two brothers and a sister, all already old it seemed to me. None of them ever married.

Catherine came to the door and tugged me inside. She held me a moment against the rough brown wool of her dress. I gave her the cookies. Everything about her was brown—hair, clothes, even her skin—and never a hint of ornamentation, no jewelry or pearls or metal buttons, nothing that would shine except her face sometimes when she'd been in the kitchen leaning over the wood-burning range. Yes, and her eyes. They would shine, coming alive suddenly when I entered the dark and musty house. Shades were drawn as though to keep out any sunlight that might fade or age some rug or piece of furniture or maybe even the three people themselves.

Donald was tall. Because of some old injury he carried his head tilted a little to one side. That gave him a stern and judging look. His hands were huge, weather-roughened knobs at the end of his arms. To shake hands with him was like taking hold of a rough-sawn two-by-four. When he saw me come in, he lifted an old phonograph onto the dining room table. It played a hollow cylinder instead of the flat records I had played on the Victrola at my mother's parents. Donald wound the crank and put a cylinder in place. The huge hand gently lowered the needle. Ancient, tinny music came out.

Riley, the older brother, paid no attention to me at all. He was talking, to himself it seemed to me, though maybe the other two had just stopped listening. He complained about his stay in a Catholic hospital in La Crosse. Especially he complained about the nurses, who were nuns, calling them "those goddamned blackbirds."

In an act of friendship, or trust, or maybe to make up for his brother's rudeness, Donald brought out a little red box. He opened the box to show me, the big hands carefully folding back the tissue paper. Inside the paper were blond ringlets of hair. He lifted them out, the ringlets curling around his fingers.

"My first haircut," Donald said.

He wrapped the ringlets again in the tissue and put them back into the red box. He did all this without a smile or any softening of his face. I could not believe he had ever been young.

Catherine came over to me, touched my shoulder and left her hand there while she said she was going to see about cookies. Even as she turned toward the kitchen, her hand lingered on my shoulder until she was an arm's length away.

Riley was still talking. The old phonograph was playing. Donald sat at the table with the red box before him.

I looked around me. It was not just Catherine who was brown. The house was dressed in brown, too. The worn rug was brown and the wainscoting that covered the lower third of the walls. Sepia-brown pictures lined the upper part, some of them stern faced portraits—old men with beards and women with tight buns of hair. Above the dining room table was a large brown-toned picture of an Indian sprawling beside his horse. The caption said: "The End of the Trail."

It was cold in the house. The woodburning stove—it was enameled brown—gave out almost no heat. What warmth there was in the room came from the kitchen where Catherine was working.

She talked to me through the open door. Finally she came out with a paper bag that was warm in my hands and smelled of molasses cookies. She smiled and handed me one cookie to eat on my way home.

I shook hands with Donald.

Catherine put her arm around me and walked close beside me out onto the porch.

"Thank you," she said. "You make it seem like Christmas."

Her hand was heavy on my shoulder. I knew she did not want me to go. I slid out from under that lingering touch and ran out the gate. I grabbed my sled rope and raced out of the barnyard, across the field toward home. At the edge of the woods, I looked back.

She was standing on the porch, watching me, a straight brown shape. I waved to her and ran into the woods.

I ran almost all the way home and rushed into the warm kitchen, all out of breath. I gave the bag of cookies to Mother.

"How's Catherine?" she asked.

I hesitated. I didn't know how to say that she was so lonely I wanted to cry, and that something in that house tried to wrap itself around me to get my warmth.

"She's all right," I said.

Mother smiled. "And she gave you a cookie to eat on the way home."

"Yes. And Donald played the old phonograph again."

"What songs?"

"Some didn't have any words. One was 'Pale hands I loved beside the Shala-something.'"

"Shalamar?" Mother asked.

"Yes. 'Pale hands I loved beside the Shalamar—where are you now—where are you now?'"

"Oh, my," Mother said. She gave me a hug. "I think you need a hot cup of cocoa."

She stood at the kitchen window and kept glancing at me as I sipped the cocoa. "Remember," she said, "they have no children to remind them of other Christmases. It is you children who do so much to help make it Christmas for your father and me."

I didn't say anything. I was thinking of that lonely house, glad I was still safe in childhood.

Suddenly Mother laughed. "You know what I like to do when I'm feeling gloomy in the dark days of winter? I look out this window and think of summer, with the days long again and the sun going high."

I joined her at the window.

"See that little hump of a hill on the horizon, way over in the southeast? That's where the sun comes up on the shortest day of the year, just before Christmas. I look at that. Then I look where the sun will come up on the longest day of the year, way over there in the northeast, just beyond the end of the tobacco shed."

I looked at the hump of a hill in the southeast, then swung my eyes along the horizon far to the left, to the end of the tobacco shed. I had not known that Mother had the travels of the sun mapped out along the horizon.

She gave me another hug. "It means a lot to Catherine, your stopping to see her at Christmas."

"I know," I said, and it was all right. I was thinking of the slow roll of the seasons around us and how the sun was a part of our lives.

It Will be Like Christmas

Blizzards were the very heart of the Wisconsin winters of my childhood, and despite the awesome power and danger of those days of storm, they gave us a hint of what Christmas is.

We liked blizzards, we four boys. The storms challenged us, made us feel like intrepid trappers or mounted policemen following a dog sled somewhere in the great barrens north of Hudson Bay.

It seems to me now that the worst winter storms always came early in the New Year when there was no warmth left in the land to temper the cold wind. I can't be sure. All the blizzards of those years have gathered into a feeling of one great classic storm that came roaring down from the north to test us and see if we could survive.

The blizzards tried to sneak up on us. It started with a wind-driven, freezing rain and a sky so gray and cold that only a fool would ever expect to see warm sunshine again. Ice coated the ground in a smooth, treacherous layer. We strapped little steel-toothed ice creepers onto our overshoes before we went out, then walked flat-footed to make sure the teeth were gouging into the ice. The only tracks we left were the tiny holes of the teeth. Mother watched us from a window, worrying that we'd fall and put similar little holes in ourselves.

The trees were covered with ice, branches cracking against each other. Long dripping icicles hung from the eaves of the buildings. The clouds were low, going very fast, and had a greenish look.

Suddenly nothing was dripping. The rain changed to tiny round bullets that stung our faces and rattled on the buildings. The windmill groaned around with its load of ice as the wind changed and came blasting straight out of the northwest. The pelting sleet changed to snow. It didn't seem to be falling at all, just flying horizontally past us in the wind. Even though the flakes were small, it was soon snowing so hard we could no longer see from the house to the barn. An angry blaze of sunset showed briefly in the west. A sundog's bright red streak stuck straight up from the horizon. Loose snow began covering the smooth ice, making it slipperier than ever, but at

4 5

least the snow was a cushion if we fell.

Father rounded us up. "Blizzard coming. Let's get our work done. Don't anybody go wandering off in this."

I gave the chickens warm water and extra feed. I carried a mountain of wood from the woodshed, piling it high on the porch and filling the space behind the kitchen stove. Sparrows were flying around the eaves, looking for shelter, some of them trying to get through the screen onto the porch. The bird feeder on the big maple tree was deserted.

The farm buildings were all that was left in the world. There were no woods to the west, no farm to the east, no other ridges to the north, no rolling fields stretching toward Lost Valley. When the snow gusted around me, only the house and woodshed stayed in sight.

I could hear someone calling. I went down past the windmill walking wide around it because of the falling ice and found Father at the chicken-house door, ear flaps down, his coat covered with white. He cupped his hands and yelled, "Tell your mother we'll go ahead and milk before supper. That way we won't have to come out again."

I nodded and ran for the house. At the porch I turned to look back. Father and the chicken house had vanished in the white. A cloud of steam came out of the kitchen when I opened the door and ducked in. The snow followed me and spit against the top of the hot stove. Mother already had a lamp on the kitchen table so it would shine out the window toward the barns. "It's like seeing a lighthouse through the storm," Father once told her. Always after that, she made sure the lamp was there on bad nights.

She brushed snow off my shoulders. "I'm glad you're not out there coming home from school in this."

I told her about supper. She nodded, thinking of the longer evening ahead. "Better start a fire in the other room."

"The other room" meant the living room, a snug room with a low ceiling in the thick-walled, log part of the house. Most evenings it stayed cold and dark. Using the short-handled fire shovel, I scooped live coals out of the dining-room stove and carried them, smoking, sparks flying, to the living-room stove. I put corncobs and small pieces of wood over the coals. Soon the fire was roaring and I opened the little metal register that let the heat go to the upstairs bedrooms.

Mother came in and sniffed the air. "Smells musty in here. Get a few more coals on the shovel."

I did that, and she sprinkled ground coffee over the coals. There were little sparkles of light as the coffee caught fire. Smoke came up and the good smell of burnt coffee spread as she walked around the room with the shovel.

"There, that's better."

The others came tramping into the kitchen, snow following them, the wind a load roar while the door was open.

"Whoosh," Father said, rubbing snow off his face. His eyebrows were white. He smiled at Mother. "You know, snow's so thick I was past the well before I could see your light."

Lyle, the hired man, stomped in and slammed the

door. He was shivering and headed for the dining room stove without even taking off his jacket. "It's the kind of night makes you wonder what you did with your summer's wages."

We gathered for supper at the dining table, stove roaring inside, wind roaring outside. The windows rattled and the whole house shook in a strong gust.

Mother looked around the table as though counting us. "I'm glad you're all inside."

So were we.

After supper, Mother made a batch of chocolate fudge. When she took it off the stove, I took the pan outside, setting it down into the soft snow that was sifting onto the porch. I let it cool, then brought it back in for her to beat and pour into a pan. I made popcorn, two heaping bowls with melted butter poured over the top. Every head in the dining room turned when I walked in with the first bowl.

Mother followed with the second bowl and the fudge. "Let's go in the other room," she said.

I lighted the pull-down kerosene lamp which had a big china shade with pale wild roses painted on it and glass prisms hanging down all around. Father came in and poked the fire. One by one everyone joined us, Lyle last of all, carrying a chair with him so he could sit close to the stove and toast his feet.

We started on the fudge and popcorn. Mother began to play the piano. In a minute Father went over and stood behind her, a hand on her shoulder. She switched to another song and he sang with her. We joined them, singing and eating at the same time.

"It'll sound better when the popcorn's gone,"

CHAPTER FIVE

Mother said.

Between songs the wind on the west side of the house was a solid roar.

Bedtime came early. We filled the heating stoves to the top of the doors with chunks of oak and closed the dampers so the fires would burn all night. The lamps were blown out, leaving a kerosene smell in the air. We went off to our beds, where mountains of quilts and blankets pushed us down deep into the mattresses. The house began to relax for the night. Floor boards popped back. Walls and ceiling creaked and groaned as the house cooled. Outside, the roar of the wind went on, gusts slamming against the siding, rattling eaves spouts and grumbling in the chimneys. Sometimes the wind fell for a moment and there was the cold and ghostly rustle of snow against the windows.

The wind was the first thing we heard when we woke the next morning. We had slept later than usual, but it was still pitch dark outside. Father called us. We waited until we heard the dining room stove roaring, then ran out there to get dressed, hoping Mother wouldn't notice we had slept in our long winter underwear instead of our flannel nightshirts.

Snow was a foot deep on the porch when we went out. Father disappeared toward the hog house carrying a smoking bucket of live coals to get a fire started in the water-tank heater. The wind blew out our lanterns before we got halfway to the barn. The drift below the milkhouse was almost to the top of the gate. The barn was warm, the cows mooing for feed and company.

We did all the chores so we wouldn't have to come

out again until afternoon then ran for the house, shielding our faces from the driving snow.

"Is it still snowing?" Mother asked.

"Can't tell," Father said, "if it's snowing or just blowing."

The blizzard went on. The stove in the other room burned all day. We were isolated. The road was drifted full. The telephone didn't ring because the ice had broken the line somewhere. We played cards and got out all of our old games. Even when we were older, a long blizzard day made us young again. We found our wooden blocks and made cities, built crazy-looking machines with tinkertoys, made long fences of dominoes. Touch the first domino and click-click-click the line collapsed, one by one, curving and circling, seeming to take forever.

"Hey! If we had enough dominoes we could build a line clear around the world. They'd go clicking-clicking out of sight to the east. About ten years later they'd come clicking-clicking back from the west."

"Wouldn't work."

"Why not?"

"What you going to do about the oceans?"

"Oh."

"Hey! Maybe we could invent a new kind of dominoes. They'd float, standing straight up. Nothing in the world could tip one over until another domino clicked against it."

We argued. We experimented in the kitchen wash basin and might have made a million dollars if we hadn't gotten the floor all wet.

Something in the blizzard made us relentlessly hungry. An hour after breakfast we were cracking and eating hickory nuts, walnuts and butternuts behind the kitchen stove, using one of Mother's heavy irons as an anvil. Lyle came padding out of the dining room in his stocking feet to watch us. He stepped on a sharp nutshell, then yelled and hopped on one foot like a chicken.

Mother always had extra books stored away for blizzards. She gave me Bambi on a day like that. When I re-read it years later, I was surprised to find it wasn't always snowing in the book.

With the doors between rooms open and all three stoves going, the whole house was warm, though the temperature could vary twenty degrees from one corner to another. We roamed restlessly from room to room. When other books ran out, we gathered in the closet at the head of the stairs and hauled out the old encyclopedias. They were leather-bound and so old we expected them to say the world was flat. Each with a volume in his lap, we competed to see who could find the most fascinating facts, never daring to invent too much on our own because someone was sure to check.

"Hey!" Lee said once. "It says Wisconsin has the winter climate of northern Sweden or central Russia."

We looked at each other and were instantly

changed. The wind was howling around us. We stood in our black bearskin caps and coats on the edge of the Bering Strait, trying to see the other side. We were caught on an ice floe. We were wrapped in quilted goosedown clothes and peering out into the storm from our igloos. Icebound explorers, we tramped onward toward the Pole, our guides turning back, our dogs frozen, food almost gone.

"Hey! When the blizzard's over let's build an igloo."

"Let's make a harness and see if Shep will pull a sled!"

"Mush!" we yelled.

"Mush, you fool dogs. There's a blizzard coming and Fort Henry's twenty miles away!"

"What's going on up there?" Mother called.

Up there? We were in the Arctic. One's mother couldn't call him in the Arctic. One's mother stayed patiently at home waiting for someone to bring word that he was dead or had triumphantly reached the Pole and would be home after a wild parade in Paris and then another in Zanzibar.

"Mush, dogs. Mush!"

"I said what's going on up there?"

"Nothing. We're just playing."

We closed the closet door and spoke in hoarse whispers. We were Royal Mounted Policemen, trailing our man up into the far reaches of the Arctic Circle, so far north it was dark all day. The smell of food brought us back from the Arctic. We ate, and Father mushed us out into the blizzard to do the chores. The drift at the fence was up to the eaves of the chicken house. We shoveled snow away from the barn doors. The cattle came out, walking stiff-legged, then stopped to lick themselves. Gathering energy, they hobbled to the tank, where the heater was smoking and the water steaming in the cold.

We finished the chores again. The thermometer on the milkhouse said ten below zero. Fine snow blew into our faces, taking our breath away so that we gasped and choked and felt as if we were drowning.

In the house, we found Mother humming a little song, looking very pleased with herself. Her cookbook was open on the kitchen table, surrounded by pans and bowls. "We're going to have a special meal to celebrate the blizzard and I need some things from the cellar," she told me.

Her happy face and request reminded me of Christmas. Once again I made my familiar expedition down through the creaking trap door, lantern flame turned up high. I hurriedly gathered up what Mother wanted. I dashed up the narrow stairs only to hear her voice say, "I forgot. Bring some apples, too."

Down again into the darkness. Then, bowl of apples in one hand, lantern in the other I ran up the steps and leaped out of the stairway.

Safe once more from whatever it is that lives and waits in dark places, I took my spoils out into the kitchen. Mother sorted through them, her face alive with pleasure.

"You're a magician," she said. "In the middle of a blizzard you bring summer up from the cellar."

The warming apples spread their smell. Soon a face appeared in the door. "Did I smell apples? Can I have one?"

The storm went on. Frost formed on all the windows, creeping along the glass, delicate, fast-growing white ferns. The crystals thickened and became lacy trees with leaves like shining fish scales. Finally there was just thick white frost with holes scraped through in special places so we could look out at the blowing snow.

Night came, then morning again, and still the roaring wind and snow went on. Father wandered restlessly, looking for something to do. Mother brought out pots that needed soldering. That done, Father would bring in broken harnesses. If the storm came when the seed corn had already been tested, we all shelled corn, our hands raw from rubbing the hard kernels off the cobs. The cobs were Father's morning kindling, though sometimes Mother rescued them and boiled them in water to make a thin, sweet corn syrup.

The roar of the wind had been around us so long we hardly heard it anymore. The sounds inside the house grew louder—the tap-tap of harness rivets, the meat saw biting into a quarter of frozen beef, the coffee grinder, someone laughing at something in a book, the creak-creak of Mother's ironing board, the slap of her hand on rising dough, the moist *bueyooey* sound of mouth-made car exhausts, a pound-pound from the kitchen that said only one thing in the world—raw beef on a wooden cutting board being pounded to make it tender. And there was Junior running a ten-penny nail up and down the strings of his guitar, trying to make Hawaiian music.

"Sounds like wolves," said Lyle.

"Ghosts," said Lee.

"Sounds like somebody running a silly nail up and down guitar strings," said Laurance.

Father cleared his throat. "Sounds unnecessary."

Junior grinned and retreated. Soon the mournful sound of his harmonica came from the living room, playing "Red River Valley," "Beautiful Dreamer," "Wabash Cannonball," "Little Red Wing," and a song that no one else remembers about a man who said he was going to the state prison at Waupun.

Once, on a day like that, I was alone in the kitchen with Father and Mother. The dog was there—all dogs were called Shep then—and he was restless, wanting to get outside and run but turned back by the cold wind every time we opened the door for him. He came over to Father, who was riveting a buckle back onto my overshoe, and put out a paw to shake hands. Father laughed and Shep began trying to play, claws slipping on the linoleum floor.

"Say," Father said, "remember when you were little? We used to get down on the floor, I and all four of you, with Shep and wrestle. Shep would growl at me when I squeezed one of you and made you yell."

I didn't remember. I had to say that.

Father looked at me, the laughter gone.

Mother came over and put her hand on his shoulder. "I think it must have been the older ones."

Father went back to tapping at the copper rivet, not noticing that Shep was trying to shake hands again. Then Father reached out and touched my shoulder. "Son, I guess a man gets so busy trying to make a living he forgets to be a father."

I wasn't good at finding the right words to say to Father, but I had to say something that would change the look on his face.

"There were other things," Mother said.

"I remember once," I said, "we were way out in the middle of the Mississippi, the two of us, in a rowboat. I was a lot younger. I thought it might be the sea."

"Did we catch any fish?"

"I don't remember. I just remember you rowing me in the rowboat."

Mother smiled at me.

"And you used to tell us about an old mill. In Norway. There was a light in a window. You and your brothers used to run to find the light and it was never there."

Father nodded. "I remember. Your eyes always got bigger than cream-can lids. Would you like to hear that story?"

"Yes."

He told it again. And he wasn't my father in the story at all. He was a young boy, no older than I, running, running in the summer of a land I had never seen.

Mother gave us both a hug and went back to her work at the kitchen table.

The day ended. By the time we came in from

chores the thermometer stood at twenty below. Lyle wrapped himself around the dining room stove and shivered. "By golly, by morning it's going to be colder than a cast iron witches' ti . . ."

I waited, but he caught himself just in time.

"Colder than a cast iron . . .ah . . .monkey wrench in Alaska."

Mother looked up from the sock she was darning. "Why, that's an odd expression. I never heard that before."

"Neither did I," Lyle said. "Made it up on the spot."

That started Lyle and Father talking about all the tales of men lost in blizzards, maybe freezing to death fifty feet from the house. Out on the Plains men strung ropes between the house and barn. Someone who was lost would run into a fence and follow it, hoping it was going toward help, not away from it. If you were lucky you ran into the side of a building and felt your way along it, looking for a corner and a door.

"Heard about a fellow who did that," Lyle said. "He froze to death anyway."

"How come?"

"Well, he kept going along that building for what seemed like a month of Sundays. Never did find the end. They found him out there next morning."

"All right. What's the catch?"

"No catch at all. It was told to me as a true story. You see that building the fellow ran into was a round barn."

The wind was suddenly gustier. As it tried to come down the chimney, puffs of smoke came out around the stove doors. At supper, a new sound came from the living room. The wind began a certain humming howl around the eaves. It made us think of ghosts and tales of Russian children being thrown one by one from a sleigh to slow up the pursuing wolves. It was a deep, throbbing howl that happened maybe once or twice a winter when the wind was very strong and coming from exactly the right direction.

We all stopped eating and waited. Then the other sound began, a fainter, vibrating imitation of the first. I felt the hair rising on the back of my neck. It was Mother's piano, playing all by itself, the strings vibrating in tune with the howling wind.

Father smiled at Mother. "Maybe it's just asking you to come play it."

After supper she did that and we sang, our voices blocking out the wind.

I woke that night, knowing something had happened. The house was so still I might have been the only person left in the world. I could feel ice against my face where my breath had frozen on the covers. Reaching one hand out into the grabbing cold, I scraped frost from the windowpane. Stars were shining. Then I knew what had awakened me. The wind was gone. The blizzard was over. I pulled my head down under the covers and went back to sleep.

The ice was a half-inch thick on the kitchen water bucket when we got up next morning. The thermometer on the milkhouse said forty-two below zero. Snow squeaked under our overshoes, the telephone wire hummed in the cold, and the big drift reached almost to the top of the chicken house roof. The sun came up, a blinding red ball, with a rainbow-colored sundog guarding it on each side. White smoke rose straight up from the neighbor's chimney, and other farms and other ridges were there again in every direction.

George Holliday came with the mail, riding on horseback, our first contact with the outside world. Late in the day, the roaring, clanking snowplow came by, throwing up snowbanks fifteen feet high along the road to the west. Despite all the activity, there was loneliness in such a day. I kept feeling I should be looking for something I had lost. I tried to talk to Mother about that. She nodded and put her arm around me. Together we stood and looked out the kitchen window. Lyle was hitching a team of horses to a sled. Father was at the door of the hog house. Laurance was shoveling snow at the barnyard gate. Lee and Junior were filling a manger with hay for the cows.

Mother sighed. "I know what you mean. The blizzard brings us together. Now we're all busy, going our own way again. I guess a blizzard spoils us a little. I guess we can't expect it to be that way all the time."

"Could we have a fire in the other room again tonight?" I asked.

She smiled. "Yes. I'll make some fudge."

"I'll make popcorn. It will be like Christmas."

"Yes," she said. "Like Christmas."

Santa Claus is a Woman

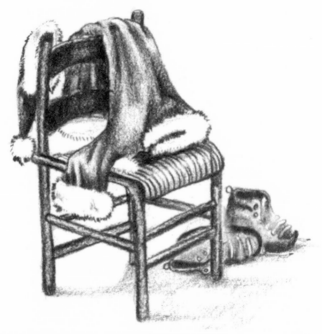

Christmas, 1937, was a bleak, lonely time. Mother had died suddenly, unexpectedly, not long after the previous Christmas. The months had crept by. The hushed and whispering feel of death had gone away, but the house stayed empty and quiet. A thousand times I had started out to look for her, to ask her something, tell her something. Even with the constant flow of the seasons to tell us that life is filled with endings and beginnings, there had been no preparation for life without Mother.

In that first winter after her death, we all seemed to be waiting for someone else to make Christmas happen. The woman who kept house for us went off to her own people. With her gone, there were the six of us—Father; Lyle, the hired man; and four boys. We realized then how much Christmas revolved around Mother. Our clumsy efforts to plan Christmas served only to help us more fully understand what we had lost. There was no atmosphere of expectation in the house, no hiding places we were not to peek into.

As the youngest, I had become, without any discussion about it, the center of the household. It fell to me to prepare a Christmas dinner. At seventeen I was not ready for that. There were questions I needed to ask her—how to roast the chickens, how long it took to bake the Hubbard squash. And dressing for the chickens. What in the world was in that? The only successes in the meal were the cranberries and the pumpkin pie. The pie, of course, had been left by the housekeeper.

Mostly I remember that Christmas as not being Christmas at all. The piano remained silent. Junior's guitar did not seem right for carols. Lyle huddled close to the dining room stove. He tried some storytelling to cheer us up, but he was grieving, too. He soon gave up and was as silent as the rest of us.

For the first time there was no letter from Father's mother in Norway. She, too, had died early in the year. Still, there was proof that families, like kings and queens and life itself, can move on past death. There was a letter from Norway, written by Seina, the wife of Father's older brother. I remember Father carrying the letter, walking from room to room as though expecting Mother to still be there. Of course, she was there, but we had trouble finding her. We talked a little about that at the dinner table, but the day remained somber.

That failure of a Christmas seemed to invite transitions.

I went off to college the next fall. Laurance, my older brother, was helping build the Mississippi dam at Lynxville. Junior went to Milwaukee to take a course in diesel mechanics, and restless Lee soon climbed into his four-cylinder Henderson motorcycle and roared off to Illinois.

I came home from college each year in those dark days of December, but we never found a way to recover Christmas. It was a casualty of her death.

I thought about those changes as our memories of how it used to be dropped further into the past. I began to realize for the first time just how much we owed her for the rituals and the special days of celebration that had lightened and brightened our lives on that farm we called Seldom Seen. It became, for me, one of those little discoveries of how things work—of how clearly it is a few special people who have the energy, tenacity and the clear vision of human possibility that can keep the spirit of Christmas alive. Christmas does not come to us just because there is a day marked in red on the December calendar. It comes to us because of women like my mother who keep hold of Christmas all year, who treasure old and valuable rituals, who somehow can make Christmas real and new each year.

It seems so obvious now, looking back. Men play Santa Claus. Women *are* Santa Claus. I think Mother would have been surprised by that idea, but she was

Santa Claus. I didn't know that until she was no longer there and we found that none of the rest of us had that special talent. She led and we joined.

There would have been nothing to join if it had not been for her.

And when the Christmas season was over, she carefully put the symbols of Christmas away. I can still see her closing the bright red paper bells and making them flat again. I can see her packing away the ornaments, holding some in her hands for a moment, her face telling me that her thoughts were with an earlier Christmas. She, more than the rest of us, knew that Christmas in not just a day, a season, or a single year. Christmas has a life of its own that persists, immune to time.

Now, when I see a man "playing Santa," I find myself thinking it should be a woman in the red suit. Because it is women, who know how to make Christmas happen.

Wartime Christmas

I was in the Navy for more than four years during World War II. In looking back now, I first told myself I have no memory of there ever being a Christmas in those years. Then, after making a list of where I had been, the details began to come back. Even in the dark seasons of war there were little incidents that provide hints of what Christmas is.

Christmas of 1942 found me in Navy Midshipman School in Chicago, quartered in Michigan Hall on what in peacetime was the Northwestern University Medical campus. Snow was falling on Christmas Eve.

I went out alone and walked for several hours in the snow, feeling alien on those city streets, cut off physically and emotionally from the hill country of Wisconsin. The good Christmases of the past seemed long ago. There was nothing in the future beyond the frightening unknowns of war. Only the falling snow, drifting along the streets and making an orange glow around the lights, was familiar and had anything to do with Christmas.

Cold and windblown, I walked back to Michigan Hall. Inside, I heard voices in song and found a group of midshipmen in the recreation room, singing carols. A blond young man was at the piano.

I recall standing for a time at the back of the room, listening. I wonder now about those young men and all the different kinds of Christmases they might have been remembering—good Christmases, bad Christmases, non-Christmases—the idea of Christmas a persistent theme but every person and family with their own accumulated memory of what it is.

I moved up close to the piano and joined the singing. Someone asked the blond midshipman, who had been with the Fred Waring Chorus, to sing a song he had written. Some of the words, as I remember them, were: "Take me down to the sea, boys. Take me down to the sea, where the waves kiss the sun, and the porpoises run, there's a job to be done, ship ahoy."

There was silence after his song. It was a reminder that this was a temporary time. In two months our training would be over and we would be scattered to the four winds.

The blond man banged the keyboard and started another carol. We went on singing. For a little time, even though we were strangers, there was a feel of Christmas in being gathered there and linking our voices in song.

A year later I was in Palermo, Sicily, a stop-over on my way from Naples to North Africa where I would be assigned to another landing craft.

There was a small officers club near the harbor. It had been an elegant house once. Red damask silk covered the walls, and there were beautifully carved faces on the heavy furniture. I went there a day or two before Christmas.

One of the officers, a lieutenant commander, had been a Hollywood actor. I played a game of pool with him and he won easily. Another officer was watching, teasing the actor about his swashbuckling film roles, saying he handled a pool cue like a sword and asking if he planned to swing from the curtains.

I lost another game.

"You are not concentrating," the commander said.

"I know," I said. "I seem to have other things on my mind."

"Like what?" He said it as though it was from a script where he had played a crusty admiral.

The other officer knew what had happened, and said, "He just lost his landing craft with everyone aboard."

The commander nodded. "Let's play," he said.

He took his shot and missed by several inches.

"Don't do that!" I said.

He looked at me for a moment, then smiled. "All right."

We finished the game. He won as usual.

We wished each other a merry Christmas, half

facetiously I think. It didn't seem like Christmas. He started to leave, then came back and gave me a ticket for an opera. "Merry Christmas," he said. This time it seemed real.

The opera was *Cavaleria Rusticana.* Even that one-act production seemed ambitious in wartime Palermo, but I had never been to an opera and was willing to do anything that would occupy my mind.

The opera house was shabby, lights dim and flickering. I remember little about the story. I just know the music was well played and that some of it seemed terribly sad.

When the lights came back up, I was crying, holding my head down, trying to hide the tears. I could not stop. A woman in the row ahead of me was watching. She reached out and touched me on the shoulder. She nodded and said something I did not understand.

I went on crying, openly now. Others were watching. They began to walk past, women and men both. Each reached out and touched me, firmly on the shoulder or lightly on the head, like a benediction. Some of them had tears in their eyes.

The people left. I sat alone, crying. It was the first time I had done that, let myself openly grieve for the men who had died on the landing craft.

At the end of the year in 1944 I was stationed ashore on a Navy Amphibious Base in Tunisia. A few days before Christmas I was ordered to do a sea-test on an LCT (Landing Craft, Tanks) that had just been repaired. There was no other officer aboard. A bearded bosun (petty officer) was in charge of the crewmen.

We fought our way out of the harbor against the incoming tide current and cruised along the North African coast toward the point called Razz Zebib. The testing took longer than I expected. The bosun thought we should do everything according to regulations. In fact, he kept reading the regulations to me, saying he wanted to be sure the LCT behaved right.

I had put in a lot of time on LCTs. They were stubborn, awkward vessels, each with a mind of its own. I told the bosun no LCT had ever behaved right in its life.

He ignored that. He read me more regulations, but finally agreed with me that the LCT was seaworthy, at least as LCTs go.

As we headed back toward the harbor, a freighter rounded the point, bound west. She was riding high in the water, which meant she was empty.

The ship swung in toward us and heaved-to. A junior officer came out on deck and hailed us, using a megaphone. "Ahoy, LCT. Can you hear me?"

I shut off the three growling diesels and yelled, "I hear you."

"We are heading home. We have a hundred cases of beer we don't need. We will sell it for one hundred dollars."

"My god," the bosun said. "That's 2400 bottles of beer."

"Stand by!" I yelled.

I counted my own money and checked with the crew. Most of them were broke.

"Forty-two bucks is all we can raise," I called. "Most of us haven't been paid for three months."

On the freighter a crewman wearing greasy dungarees ran up the ladder and talked with the hailing officer. An older man, wearing the four stripes that identified him as the captain, came on deck and joined the conversation. In a minute he took the megaphone from the other officer.

"Forget the forty-two bucks," the captain called. "I've just been reminded it's almost Christmas. Come alongside. You can have it."

The bosun was muttering. I think he was saying he didn't believe any of this was happening.

We came alongside the freighter. A boom swung out. A cargo net with the hundred cases of beer was slowly lowered to the deck of the LCT. The awed crew began unloading the cargo net. I don't think any of us had ever seen that much beer in one place.

The men of the freighter lined the rail, grinning down at us. "Merry Christmas," one of them called. There was a chorus of Merry Christmases.

"Captain," the bosun said. He was having trouble with his voice. "Captain, I'll always think of Santa Claus as wearing gold stripes."

"Hell," the captain growled, "it was the crew's idea. Isn't that something? Well, enjoy it. We need to get underway."

"Say hello to the States for us," an LCT crewman called.

"Where you headed?" another asked.

"It's supposed to be a military secret," the captain said. "But is anyone down there from around New York City?"

Two men yelled yes.

"Anybody you want me to call?"

The two men each gave him a name and telephone number.

"Captain," one of them said, "I'd just as soon you didn't mention the beer. That's my mother. I'm only seventeen. She doesn't know I drink."

"Right," the captain said. "I'll tell her your character is intact."

There were yells of Merry Christmas again. We pulled away toward the harbor. The freighter swung back to the open sea and headed toward home.

The hundred cases of beer looked very conspicuous on the open deck. I decided we had not fully enough tested the repaired LCT. There had been no trial landing on the beach. We ran the bow up onto the sand. There, hidden from the Naval base by the hulk of a torpedoed merchant ship, we broke open one of the cases of beer. We each had one, including the seventeen-year-old who, despite his age, had already participated in the two largest amphibious landings in history.

I reminded the bosun that alcoholic beverages are not supposed to be consumed on U.S. Navy vessels. The bosun sipped his beer and seemed to be thinking about that. I already knew he had a serious fault—a habit of reading naval regulations. This time the fault proved helpful. I swear he said these exact words:

"As I recall, Sir, regulations say no alcoholic beverages on ships. This is a craft, not a ship. I also suggest, Sir, that the regulations mean commissioned vessels. LCT's are listed as vessels in *service*."

The crewmen were nodding.

The bosun was not finished. He pointed out that the bottles of beer were not labeled.

"You mean we could say we didn't know what it was. We could say it looked like a soft drink."

"Exactly," he said. "Anyway, Sir, if beer is not hard liquor, then it has be soft, doesn't it?"

That seemed to take care of naval regulations.

There was still the question of distribution. The generosity of the merchant ship was contagious. Each of us would get a half-case of beer. Then, by common agreement, we decided to parcel out the rest to all the other landing craft that were in port.

We did that and told each crew the whole story. By the time we finished, we had each begun to feel like Santa Claus, and there was a feel of Christmas among the ships.

The beer was apparently consumed with discretion. No higher officer ever mentioned it. Next time I saw the bosun he told me someone had come over to his LCT and run a red and white stocking cap up the flag line to hang just under the stars and stripes.

The cap hung there until a high ranking staff officer saw it and said it was "inappropriate." He ordered the bosun to take the cap down, obviously having no idea what it stood for in this case. Somehow, that made the whole story even better.

There was another odd happening that same Christmas. My officer's quarters roommate, Harry Souchon, was a central figure.

Harry was from New Orleans. He was a dapper, playful-minded man whose moods could swing in moments from happy to sad. He missed his wife and children and, like a lot of us during the war, he drank a bit too much.

Harry had a taste for good wine and brandy and had discovered a source. Some miles out into the Tunisian Plains was a group of White Friars. Their vineyard had not been totally destroyed by the war. The Friars—we called them Brothers—made wine and a fine liquor called Eau de Vie de Vin. It was distilled from white wine, was almost clear, had a wine-like aroma and a reasonably gentle taste. That was deceiving.

We went quite often to make purchases from the Friars, and became accustomed to seeing a group of sad-faced little boys at the place. Harry had become good friends with Brother Armand who told us the children were war orphans from destroyed villages. The friars were trying to help them. We always said hello to the boys. The frozen faces did not respond.

"They are driven inside themselves," Brother Armand told us. Just before Christmas he asked Harry to play Santa for the boys.

Harry agreed. A much too large Santa suit was found somewhere. Early on Christmas Eve, as Harry was getting dressed for the event, he began thinking of his own family. He opened a bottle of Eau de Vie and poured himself a large drink. He finished dressing. A pillow was wedged into the top of the trousers at the front. By then several drinks of Eau de Vie had been consumed.

We drove out to the Friars. The children were lined up on chairs at the front of a small room. Brother Armand told them Santa was coming.

Harry wandered in uncertainly, a bag of presents over his shoulder. His pillow was already slipping. In his excellent French he began telling the story of The Night Before Christmas. His voice, upbeat and energetic at first, soon slowed and ran down toward somber.

He stopped talking. He stood looking at the boys. Then Santa Claus began to cry. "I'm sorry," he said. "I'm sorry. I haven't seen my children for three years."

He dropped the bag of presents and walked up close to the chairs, looked down at one of the boys and said, "I have a son who was your age last time I saw him."

Harry was still crying.

A tear rolled down the face of the boy. He wiped it away roughly. His shoulders began to shake. Some of the other boys were crying.

Harry looked at Brother Armand and raised his hands in a gesture of total despair. "I'm sorry," he said. "I'm sorry. I didn't mean to spoil their Christmas."

The boy Harry had spoken to got up and wrapped his arms around Harry's legs, his face buried against the Santa suit. He was sobbing.

Other boys gathered around Harry, some hugging his legs, some just crowding close to him. Many of them were crying.

The Friars seemed immobilized.

Finally, Harry carefully freed himself from the arms of the boys. He ran awkwardly out of the room, Santa suit flapping, the pillow gone all the way down inside the baggy trousers which he held up with one hand as he retreated.

I threaded through the tight huddle of crying children and ran after Harry. When I got outside, our jeep was gone. Brother Armand came after me, a strange look on his face.

"He's gone," I said. "I'm very sorry about how it turned out. Harry is very emotional."

"Of course he is," Brother Armand said, almost snapping at me. "He is French! Come. We must find him."

We got into the old truck the Friars used in the vineyard and drove to the Navy base. Harry was in our room, sitting on the bed in his Santa suit. He was still crying. When he saw Brother Armand he began apologizing again.

By now Brother Armand was crying too. "No, no, no!" he said. "We had almost given up. We have been trying to teach them to be happy. We should have been doing what you did, teach them to cry! I tell you it is a miracle from God!"

Brother Armand kissed Harry on each cheek and handed him a bottle of Eau de Vie de Vin. He wished us both a Merry Christmas and went out of the room, shaking his head, saying "It is a miracle—a miracle."

The Time Santa Came to See Father

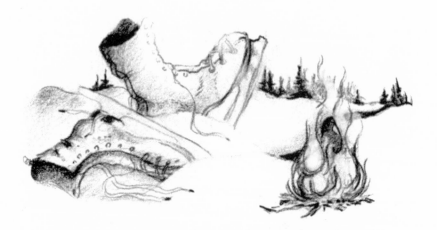

Something in the celebration of Christmas invites chaos and disaster, as though there has to be an opposite to the reverence. Someone once suggested that it's like even God gets tired of all the piety and He lets the devil win some of the time.

Christmas trees were always falling down. Unsupervised children munched on ornaments.

Santa's pillow-paunch was always slipping. Dogs wandered into school Christmas programs. The children forgot their lines and substituted something highly inappropriate.

Church Christmas programs were not immune to the chaos. Such events can simply take on a life of their own. A friend, who is a United Methodist minister, found this out. He agreed to play the role of a beggar for the church program. At the proper moment he was to shuffle up the aisle, awed by the splendor of candles and decorations, stare down for a reverent moment into the manger at the baby Jesus, and say something appropriate to the occasion.

Rehearsals went as planned, but a dew days before Christmas the minister came down with a serious case of the flu. On the night of the program he had a raging fever and hardly knew what was going on. The family left him in bed in the parsonage, next to the church.

Events proceeded without him, the performers prepared to skip the scene where the minister was supposed to enter. But right on cue, dressed in his beggar clothes, he appeared, shuffling along the aisle, staring vacant-eyed around the church, truly seeming a stranger.

There was total silence as he shuffled up to the front. Weaving unsteadily, he peered for a long time into the manger. Then he slowly turned and stared at the congregation, eyes blinking. His mouth moved and no sound came out. Finally he said, "He's—he's. He's a scrawny little devil, isn't he."

He lowered his head and seemed to be looking at his clothes in confusion. He looked again at the people and said, in a monotone, "I don't think I should have said that."

Then he turned and, using the ends of the pew

backs to steady himself, shuffled back down the aisle and out the door. He returned to the parsonage, crawled into bed and went to sleep.

The silence persisted in the church. People looked at one another. Was it funny or was it some serious theological breach? Then, one person began to clap his hands. Others followed until everyone was clapping and soon that sound was joined by raucous laughter.

The minister, of course, denies the whole event, claiming he remembers nothing about it. No matter. For that community a new and often to be repeated story of Christmas had been born.

The time Santa came to visit my father was like that.

It happened in a year long after Mother had died. Father had remarried, had rented out the farm, and was living in the little town of Blue River. The Christmas season that year was filled with promise. I had come back from my wanderings as a seaman on merchant ships. My brother Lee was there with his wife, Millie, and their two young children.

Millie was a lovely and definite Englishwoman with clear ideas about Christmas and some doubts about the ability of Americans to "do Christmas properly."

Father, that evening, had just ended a noisy session with the two children in his lap and was deep into a Zane Gray western novel which he said he had to finish "to see what happens."

There was a loud knock. The door crashed open and Santa Claus stumbled in. He pushed past the open-mouthed children, walked up to Father and clapped him on the back. "Hello there, Sam!" he said in a loud voice. "How the hell are you?"

Santa pulled a chair up close to Father. "You know, Sam, I was just thinking about that time we all went fishing for a week on the Wisconsin River. Remember, nobody wanted to be cook. So we drew lots for the first meal and said the first one to complain about the food had to cook from then on. Well, Boots got the short straw. He put about half a pound of salt into the stew. You took a bite and spit it out and said 'My god, that's salty!' Then you remembered and you said 'But that's just the way I like it.' Remember that?"

Father was nodding and laughing. Santa was laughing and clapping Father on the back again. There was a strong smell of whiskey in the room. The children were staring at Santa. Millie was momentarily immobilized. It was her first American Christmas and I resisted whispering to her that this was the way we always did Christmas in Wisconsin.

Santa, we learned later, had been at a community gathering to hand out gifts to the children. Then, without changing clothes, he had gone to the tavern where people had found some impish pleasure in buying drinks for Santa Claus.

After quite a while in the tavern, Santa had come to see Father.

The storytelling went on. Both Father and Santa seemed oblivious to Millie's dark glances and the presence of the children. The two men were busily visiting the past. They covered Halloween pranks such as putting buggies up on barn roofs, calling on girls in sleighs, then back to fishing.

"Say, Sam," Santa said, "That same fishing trip, there was this game warden came by. We played some kind of trick on him. Who was that?"

"That was D. M. Cranston," Father said. "He was Stella's father."

Stella Cranston, of course, became my mother.

"My god, Sam," Santa said. "She was such a beauty, Stella was. I still remember that time we had a big bonfire going someplace on the Pine River. It was all frozen over. We was trying to learn to skate. She was sitting by the fire, her hands tucked inside a black fur muff. She was laughing at us. She wouldn't help us learn how to skate because she said then she wouldn't have the fun of seeing us fall down."

"We were married that year," Father said. "On Christmas Day."

Santa was still. For a moment the presence of Mother was in the room and all the memories of her on other Christmases.

Millie decided it was time. She went to Santa, smiled at him, helped him up and suggested that perhaps he needed to be off to deliver presents to children who were waiting all over the world.

Santa looked at Millie blankly. He stared down at this red suit, pushed at his white beard, seeming confused, as though he had forgotten he was supposed to be Santa. The he bowed to Millie, a little wobbly, touched each child on the head and left, calling back from the door, "Merry Christmas!" The door closed. From the outside his voice came back one more time. "You take care of yourself, Sam."

Millie gathered the two children close to her, prepared to repair disillusionment. But it was all right. Ginny, the oldest grandchild, said in an awed voice, "I didn't know Granddaddy knew Santa Claus."

Father picked up his book, unaware of any tensions in the room or of any contradictions. He was smiling. The book was up in front of his face but he was looking somewhere beyond, seeming very pleased to have been reminded of those earlier days.

My memory of the time Santa came to see my father would not be the same without the presence of the children. They gave the event its definition, showing us how it is children who can rise above logic and see the wonder of Christmas. Children know things we adults cannot quite remember. Or is it that most of us have simply forgotten *how* to remember?

The question reminds me of other glimpses I have had as an adult into the minds of children. The glimpses tell me there is much confusion about Christmas. They also tell me there is poetry and meaning in the so-called confusion.

A friend was working on a script for a religious TV program. His young daughter asked what he was doing. To tease her, he said, "I'm writing about the incarnation. Do you know what that is?"

"Of course," she said. "It's a pink flower."

Well, why not? A pink carnation is a gift of life, too, isn't it?

One of my nieces once came to her mother and said, "All right. If Jesus was born at Christmas and died at Easter, where was he on the Fourth of July?"

Some of my film work used art drawn by children. One child drew four stick figures. He identified them as his father and mother, and his grandparents. Then he volunteered: "Grandparents are better than parents. They don't own you the way parents do."

Another child drew two women sitting at a table with cups in their hands. "Any time you want a grownup," she said, "they are either talking on the telephone or having coffee."

For one production, we asked first and second graders in a church school to draw pictures and talk about Christmas. The results were again confusing, and, for some church members, even disturbing.

A girl drew two adults and a child looking into the manger, with a bright star shining above. She said, "This is Mary, Joseph and Jesus looking at the new baby."

Another drawing depicted two wise men on their camels. We asked if there wasn't supposed to be three wise men. "Yeah," the boy said, "But I didn't have room for the third camel."

Some glimpses were darker. A girl drew a picture of her worst Christmas—an infant crying wildly in a high chair. She said it was the time the baby spilled gravy all over the dining room rug and her mother just screamed and screamed.

A drawing of Santa Claus was faceless. "I like Santa," the boy said. "But for me Santa doesn't have any face. There are too many store Santas. I don't know what the real one looks like."

Some of the children thought we adults asked very dumb questions. There was a drawing of three children lined up in chairs, looking at a deserted piano. The child said, "On Christmas my two sisters and I sit by the piano while my mother plays Christmas music." We asked why no one was playing. "Well," she said. "She's not at the piano yet because she's in the kitchen stuffing the turkey."

A picture of a little building showed an angel inside, floating up against the ceiling. The child explained: "An angel is in the stable instead of Jesus because she's so happy."

And there was a drawing of a person riding on a horse-like animal. The young artist said, "Mary got to ride the donkey because she's going to have the baby."

That started a discussion:

"Jesus got the horse, the donkey, the bird and the lamb."

"My cousin got a horse because he lives on a farm and was old enough."

"I always think of reindeers at Christmas."

"Did Jesus get a reindeer?"

"I don't think so."

In one picture, a happy-looking boy, arms raised to the sky, is surrounded by hundreds of snowflakes. "There has always been snow at Christmas," the artist said. "It snows and snows and snows."

A child drew a picture of himself blowing a whistle. "I got a big green whistle," he said. He paused and thought for a moment. "But a green whistle can't sing 'Glory be to God.' All a whistle can do is whistle."

My favorite drawing was a sheet of paper colored from edge to edge in solid blue. The girl said it was the blue blanket that hung over the opening to the living room when her parents were in there "fixing up" Christmas. "The best thing about Christmas," she said, "is when the blue blanket comes down."

Can we adults ever fully recover and understand those wonderfully confusing early Christmases? Maybe Robert Lewis Stevenson told us the answer in the final section of his *A Child's Garden of Verses*, where he looks back at his childhood:

Can I get there by candlelight?
So goes the old refrain.
I do not know—perchance you might—
But only children hear it right.

Mexican Posada– Is There any Room at the Inn?

In my wandering days after WW II, I spent several years in Mexico. On the surface my purpose was to study creative writing and anthropology at the

University of the Americas, but my quest was more complicated than that. Mexico City had become a haven for American veterans. We seemed to be marking time, waiting for something to gather us and set us in motion as war had done. Wars can begin instantly. Peace cannot. We carry our wars onward inside us and what we call peace is an eerie quiet where there is too much time to think and remember.

During my first Christmas in Mexico City I was invited to a party at the home of an American woman who had lived there for years. The occasion was a Posada. Starting on December 16th, these colorful reenactments of the Biblical search for room at the inn are at the heart of Mexico's Christmas season.

The wings of the woman's house enclosed a large patio with many doors leading inside, perfect for the procession of the Posada. Guests of all ages line up and go from door to door, singing the "Posada Pidienta" song (asking for lodging), each person carrying a lighted candle. Two children usually lead, carrying a litter with a clay figurine of Joseph and of Mary riding a donkey. At each door, an innkeeper (or several persons) sings his refusal. Finally, at the last door the pilgrims are allowed to enter.

I stood by myself and watched the confusion in the patio. There was laughing and joking back and forth as the procession was being organized. The woman who lived there came and stood beside me. She had a strong, somber face, her eyes very alive. "Why aren't you joining in?" she asked.

"I don't know," I said. I looked down at the drink I held. "Maybe I do. It reminds me of Italy."

She waited.

"I was there, during the war. It reminds me of that."

She waited.

"Almost all the time Italy was a sad place—bombed-out buildings, no lights. And the children, their ragged clothes, bellies swollen from hunger, hands out for help, faces that looked too old for their bodies."

I took a sip of my drink. "But sometimes at night there were open fires in the streets of a little village or a city—often where fallen walls made a shelter from the wind that blew down from the mountains. Around the fires there was sometimes happy-sounding music, even happy-sounding voices."

"I don't understand what that has to do with a Posada," the woman said.

"It seemed made up. Like they were pretending the war hadn't happened. Or like they hadn't found out yet that nothing was ever going to be the same again."

The woman sighed and touched my arm. Like a mother, I thought, who wants to help. I didn't want any help.

"You sound like my son," she said. "He won't tell me much. I think nothing had prepared him for what people do to each other in the name of war. He kept trying to figure out how people could be protected from their ability to destroy each other. Now he doesn't think anyone can be trusted with freedom."

She looked out over the patio. The procession was still getting organized. People were now chanting the rhythmic litany that was part of the Posada song as they fastened the figures of Joseph and Mary on a tray held by the children.

"My son is the ultimate casualty of the war," she said. "He went off to fight the Nazis and he came back a fascist."

I could understand someone beginning to feel that way. "War is a beast," was a phrase I had learned from an Italian woman who had not joined the happy-sounding gatherings in the streets.

"I didn't mean that," I said. "That's not how I felt in Italy. There just seemed to be something pathetic about people trying to be happy then, not facing up to the truth of war."

She was waiting again, like someone who had been to "good listening" classes.

"But my God, what do I know about anything? This is the first time I ever tried to explain it."

The woman pointed to a door. "He's inside, drinking. Would you go see him? He might talk to you about the war."

"All right," I said.

I found him slumped almost out of sight in a deep leather chair, staring into the flames in the tiled fireplace. There was a drink in his hand, a half-empty bottle of Scotch beside him. He was a medium-tall man who looked a lot like his mother but lacked the aliveness of her eyes. His hair was uncombed and he seemed too young to have been in the war. He looked up at me and waved toward the bottle. "Have some."

"I'm drinking tequila."

He made a face and pointed toward a cabinet. "You'll find some over there."

I helped myself.

He watched me. "Why aren't you out there celebrating the coming of the Nocha Buena, the good night that's supposed to answer all questions."

"I didn't feel like celebrating, either."

He straightened up in the chair and glared at me. "I suppose you've been talking to my mother. I suppose she told you I don't have much hope for the future of gallant humanity."

I nodded. I repeated what I had told her about Italy.

He poured more Scotch into his glass. "So where the hell do you pin your hopes for the future?"

"I don't know. I'm waiting to find that out while I try to come all the way home from the war."

"And just how do you do that?" The way he said it made it into an angry and sarcastic challenge. It was the first time it had occurred to me that there might be something adolescent about all of us who still seemed dominated by what had happened to us in the war. As though war had interrupted our development and left us stuck in a limbo, only half grown-up.

I thought of Italy again. "Maybe I'm not so different from the Italians as I figured," I said. "Maybe that ability they have for stealing moments of happiness in the ruins is the best symbol of hope there is."

He shook his head, slumped back in the chair and sipped at his drink. "Army?" he asked.

"Navy. Landing craft."

"Where?"

"Sicily. Then the Italian mainland at Salerno and behind-the-lines landings along the coast. Then Anzio."

"I was Army. Infantry. Normandy and all the way to the end."

He glared at me again. "Ever kill anybody?"

"Not like in the infantry. We do it differently in the Navy. We shoot down airplanes, not pilots. Sometimes, by mistake of course, our own planes. We blow up enemy ships, not crews. I said that to a Navy doctor once. He told me that was denial. He said death is what war is all about. He said thinking about war without thinking about death is like expecting to have Thanksgiving dinner without killing the turkey."

The young man laughed. For the first time his eyes were like his mother's. "So how are we supposed to do it? Come all the way back from the war?"

"I guess just time." I thought of his mother listening to me. "Maybe talking about it sometimes, too."

The procession had started in the patio. The flicker of candle light came through a window. The voices were halfway between chanting and singing.

In the name of Heaven
I beg for lodging.
For she cannot walk,
My beloved wife.

As the procession reached the first door, I could hear the innkeeper's reply.

This is not an inn
So keep on going.
I cannot open;
You may be bad people.

The flicker of candles told us the procession was moving on to another door.

Don't be inhuman;
Have mercy on us.
The God of the heavens
Will reward you for it."

And the innkeeper answered:

Better go on
And don't molest us,
For if I become angry
I will beat you up.

The young man sank back in the big chair, holding his glass in both hands. "So, doesn't it make you angry, too, all that simplistic innocence?"

"I'm withholding judgment while I sort myself out," I told him. "In the meantime I guess it beats the alternatives."

He dismissed that with a wave of his hand. We were silent and the sound of the Posada came into the room again.

We are worn out
Coming from Nazareth.
I am a carpenter.
My name is Joseph.

The innkeeper sang his refusal again:

Your name doesn't matter.
Let me sleep
For I am telling you
We shall not open.

"Merry Christmas," I said to the young man, smiling at the irony of that for both of us.

I went outside and closed the door behind me. His mother saw me and stepped out of the procession. I answered her look with that most elegant of Mexican gestures, the spread hands and shrug that said, "Who Knows?"

The procession moved on and again no one was allowed to enter. I heard the door open behind me. He was standing there, blinking in the lights, glass still in his hand. The woman came to her son, carrying two lighted candles. She put one into his hand, took his arm and pulled him across the patio and into the end of the procession. He walked with the others, carrying the drink in one hand, the candle in the other. He raised them both up for me to see and shook his head. Disbelief? Acceptance? I didn't know.

I picked up a candle and joined the line.

The children carrying the figures of Mary and Joseph stopped at another door. This time the door swung wide and the innkeeper sang:

Is it you, Joseph?
Your wife is Mary?

Enter, pilgrims,
I did not know you.

The tempo of the voices changed to a triumphal march as the children moved through the door. The procession followed until we were all inside. Mary and Joseph were placed in a miniature manger scene on a table and we stood in a circle around them, our candles filling the room with yellow light.

I knew there would be Posadas in other homes during the season. On Christmas Eve, the Niño Dios (the baby God) would be placed in the manger with Mary and Joseph, the final part of a ritual that has been going on for centuries.

I did not again see the young man who had come back from the war with trust in people gone out of him. I don't know what he found. I do know that as time passed most of the restless veterans in Mexico drifted one by one back to previous lives or on to something more real than that period of marking time when each of us looked for a way of making peace with ourself.

The Posada became a small clue for me. Such rituals, even when taken lightly, can open doors in the mind. Rituals do not persist simply because they may possess a magical power from outside us. They live because they touch something inside us that is wanting and waiting to come out and express itself.

Christmas at Rancho Don Tomas, 1953

There were four of us on the lower slopes of the steep, wooded mountainside in that remote part of the Mexican state of San Luis Potosi. Below us in the narrow valley was the tiny village of Micos, where morning smoke lifted straight up from thatched-roof buildings. Near the village was Rancho Don Tomas, the ranch house surrounded by bright splashes of red on ten-foot-high wild poinsettia bushes. Close to the mountainside on the other side of the valley I could see the blue-green of the river. From downstream came the murmur of the falls where the river tumbled down toward the more level lands, far below. Old maps labeled that cut in the mountains "The Pass of the Gentlemen Bandits."

This was on the day before Christmas during my second year in Mexico, my first Christmas ever in a tropical setting. I was a tag-along with the other three young men. We were looking for a Christmas tree.

"How do you do that in a land of palm trees?" I had asked.

One of the young men laughed and held up a hatchet. "You'll see."

The others had been there before and had links with the ranch. I was the outsider and knew they were playing a game with me. Already that morning one of them had picked and handed to me what looked like a beautifully ripe tangerine, but when I put the first section into my mouth, it was so bitter and lemon-sour that I had spit it out. They laughed at me of course.

We paused on the mountainside to listen to the raucous braying of a burro in the village, the sound echoing and re-echoing across the valley. "Mamma Grande says there used to be monkeys here," one of the young men said. "She says that's why the village is called Micos." He laughed. "But I don't know about her stories."

"Hey!" another young man said. "There's the one we're looking for."

I could see nothing that looked like a Christmas tree.

We moved forward and they showed me and all laughed at me again. It was a wild lemon tree about seven feet tall, its thick, dark green leaves shining in the sun. We cut the tree and took turns carrying it down to the ranch house where we set it up close to the fireplace, the four of us arguing, as my brothers and I had done, about how long the crossed boards at the base needed to be.

That was the beginning of an odd Christmas season. I had walked into something I knew nothing about—how Americans in another country find ways to keep the past and their own customs alive. The idea had such links with my studies in anthropology that I felt I should be taking notes. In fact, I tried to do that. The notes were a jumble. The people, the setting, the sweep of time I felt there, became a story impossible to capture.

Four generations of that family were gathered for Christmas, coming from Mexico City, California and different parts of Texas. The woman who lived at the ranch was the matriarch, the one who became the center of the season. And there were her children, her grandchildren, her great grandchildren. Everyone called her "Mamma Grande." She had been born in 1881.

When the wild lemon tree was set up and turned and tilted and moved back and forth to almost everyone's expectations, Mamma Grande took charge. Out came the old decorations—flood-stained ornaments, insect-chewed ropes that were faded to pink, a star dulled by mildew for the top of the tree. Mamma Grande handed them to us to hang on the tree, sometimes cradling an ornament in her hands as though it became a crystal ball revealing the past. The look on her face reminded me of my mother.

As I watched Mamma Grande making Christmas happen, I learned something else. Working most closely with her, seeming to know exactly what to do without being told, was her granddaughter, Jacqueline.

Jacqueline was a college student at the University of the Americas where I, too, was taking courses. We had become good friends and she had invited me to the ranch for Christmas. I knew she had lived many of her younger years at the ranch with her grandparents. I had not realized that she and her grandmother shared such a closeness, each seeming to know what the other was thinking.

From Jacqueline I had already learned some of the history of the ranch. Mamma Grande had been Mary Esther Carter and grew up in Red River County, Texas. In 1906 she married childhood sweetheart Thomas Lincoln Cowan, and on her wedding day started a journey to Mexico to become part of a colony of Americans who owned land there.

"Why Mexico?" I asked Mamma Grande.

"By the turn of the century there was no more West to go to, so we went south," she said.

That phrase, "Turn of the century," was one I had heard in my childhood, often in stories of the past that told me Americans were restless people, forever tearing up roots and scattering themselves across the land. Something in that had seemed sad to me as a child. I wondered then if those who had vanished to the West knew they were remembered in family stories.

Christmas at Rancho Don Tomas, named for Thomas Cowan, was a time of such stories, with Mamma Grande often the storyteller. For twenty years she and Thomas Cowan struggled to survive the great revolution that swept through Mexico. It was a time of chaos, with constant raids by bandits, soldiers and revolutionists. Guns were hidden in cabinets that had hidden compartments behind hidden compartments. Horses, mules and cattle were shot or stolen. The ranch house was burned, with explosions from the hidden guns and ammunition, everything else already stolen if it could be carried off on horseback. There were no cattle or horses left to sell, no way to market the sugarcane. The American colony broke up during the revolution. Much of the land was abandoned and many of the people the Cowans knew were gone.

Hurricanes came into the valley from the Gulf of Mexico. The great flood of 1933 swept the valley almost clean. Mamma Grande told of escaping to the mountains and looking down into that water-filled valley where one of her children was buried. (He had died of snake bite.) "I watched our house and all in it give up and leave for the Gulf of Mexico," she said. "All my treasures gone to the Gulf."

Mamma Grande sat quietly for a moment.

"What happened then?" someone asked.

"Only one thing to do," she said. "Close the doors of memories. Go on from there."

The house had been rebuilt. The struggle to make a living from the ranch went on.

"What happened to Grandpa Cowan?" a child asked.

"He died in 1949 of undulant fever. He is in the American Cemetery in Mexico City—a long way from Red River County." Again there was a pause. "There comes a time when one has to go out and close the door. That is over."

She might have been lecturing me about moving on from the war.

Mamma Grande stayed on the ranch after Thomas Cowan died, running the place herself. "Every day was a race with the sun," she said. "All I knew about managing a ranch was that water runs downhill."

On Christmas morning, Mamma Grande was in firm command, marshaling her troops like a military officer. Kenneth, her son, led a platoon of children outdoors to look for fruit, some of it surely out of season, but that didn't matter because the real agenda was to keep the children out from underfoot. They did have specific orders to gather oranges "before the cussed big grackles stick their bills into them and suck out the juice."

We picked great bouquets of poinsettias and carried in palmlog wood for the fireplace. We kept children from falling into the river, aided in that task by tales of lurking alligators.

Once, as I passed the kitchen, I heard Mamma Grande's raised voice saying, "Eighty-nine thousand quadrillion gol-darns!" Then I heard Jacqueline say that I was good at fixing things. I was summoned, handed an offending eggbeater with a loose handle. When that was fixed, dozens of objects needing repair came out of a jammed-full little room called "Bluebeard's Closet." On a high shelf was a tiny museum of pre-Columbian artifacts that had been found along the river—pottery bowls, pots, figurines, and cutting tools and arrowheads made from the volcanic glass called obsidian.

As I worked, I could hear voices from the kitchen, Mamma Grande and her Mexican cook speaking a bewildering combination of Spanish and English. Jacqueline was working with them, seeming perfectly at ease with that homemade language as she quizzed the two of them about the recipe for General Diaz cake, which I gathered had been served long ago when the General visited the ranch.

Several times, Mamma Grande's two daughters came into the kitchen with suggestions that all began with "Now Mamma . . ." And Mamma chased them out with a buzzing "*Tut-tut-tut-tut-tut-tut*" that reminded me of an annoyed bird.

The daughters' search for something necessary to do finally put them in charge of boiling drinking water that I suspected had been boiled once already.

During a break from my work of fixing things, I pulled a book about Mexico from the shelf. It had Mamma Grande's name in it and on many pages were her handwritten comments, all with exclamation marks: "Ha!" "He hasn't been here!" "Rubbish!" "What does he know!" and "Wrong!"

While I was looking at the book, a crying child, who had escaped from the outdoor platoon, complained loudly to Mamma Grande about some toy that had been left behind in California. She put her arm around him, listened for a moment and said, "Is this something you can do anything about?"

The child shook his head.

"Then forget it," she said.

The boy looked startled.

She pointed outside. "The sun is shining. There's a sandpile out there. Why don't you go out and play?"

Suddenly she laughed. "Do you know, a batch of children were playing out there once. I heard all this yelling. I went running out, and guess what? They had uncovered a bunch of turtle eggs. Some were hatching. Those little tiny turtles headed straight for the river. We would turn them around and they just turned right back toward the river."

The boy had stopped crying. "How do they know to do that?"

She put her hand on his head. "They just do."

The boy ran outside to the sandpile. She watched him from the doorway for a moment, then turned back into the room. She walked past me, unseeing, and went to the Christmas tree where she stood touching an ornament as though it might help her look all the way back to Texas.

On Christmas night, tall candles were lighted in the old branding irons on the mantle. Palmlogs blazed in the fireplace. We lighted the small candles on the tree. My father would have approved; the green leaves of the lemon tree could not catch fire.

There was a raw chill in the wind that blew out of the North and grumbled in the fireplace chimney. Someone joked that the cold wind was a Christmas present from Texas. That started someone else talking about the area upriver where the water fell down from the plateau known as the Mal País, "the bad country."

A child's eyes widened all round at the words.

There was talk of the cave where bandits had lived a life of leisure. They waited above the river until a line of pack mules, bound for Tampico, came to the ford with silver from the mines of San Luis Potosi. Then, these "Gentlemen Bandits," who had given the pass its name, walked down the hillside and stole the silver.

"Is some of the silver still hidden in the cave?"

"People think so," Mamma Grande said.

"Did you ever look for the treasure?"

She laughed and said, "I didn't have time to try to get rich."

Then she told the tale of another lost treasure, that of Emperor Maximilian, the Austrian placed in power over Mexico by the French in 1864. When the forces of Benito Juarez reclaimed the government, a mule train carrying Maximilian's treasure fled toward the Gulf of Mexico, the Juaristas in pursuit. Somewhere in the mountains, not far from the land that became Rancho Don Tomas, the packtrain was about to be overtaken. Some of the men went off the trail and buried the treasure. Those men were killed in the battle that followed. The treasure was never found and the richness of it grew with each telling of the tale.

Two men from the valley had spent their whole lives searching for the treasure. "Foolish men," Mamma Grande said. "Neither one of them was much of a much."

Then, an unlikely story of a jeep jolting across the river on a palmlog bridge. When the wheels suddenly dropped into a wide space between the logs, a young baby was bounced out of the jeep. It fell and teetered on the very edge of the bridge. A vaquero (cowboy) was following on his horse. He raced across the bridge, leaned from the saddle at full gallop and snatched up the baby just as it tumbled toward the river.

The doubts of the listeners were squelched by Mamma Grande's son, Kenneth. "Improbable but true," he said. "All true."

"Did you ever see a monkey here?" one of the young men asked, smiling, laying a trap for her.

She thought a moment. "I only remember seeing two. That was a long time ago. They were tailless monkeys, you know."

The young man raised his hands in defeat.

She started another story by saying it had happened about the same time the big pot fell off the kitchen range and landed on and killed a goose.

Hoots and laughter interrupted her story.

"A goose? In the kitchen?"

She could not remember why a goose had been in the kitchen. Maybe to protect it from coyotes. Or from bandits. Or from soldiers who were also bandits. Maybe from the big jaguars that sometimes came down into the valley. "And you know," she said, "there were two Bengal tigers up in the mountains."

It was too much for the skeptical young man. He tried again. "I suppose you're going to tell us those tigers walked from India across Europe, swam the Atlantic and strolled into Mexico?"

There was laughter. The young man looked pleased with himself. Mamma Grande patted his hand. "There was a train wreck. The train was carrying a circus. The tigers escaped and I won't even tell you what happened to the elephant." She waved a hand toward the mountains. "Some people say the tigers are still up there."

While the others began a lengthy discussion about the accuracy of the story and how long Bengal tigers could live in the cold of the mountains, I was thinking my own thoughts. Mamma Grande's talk became another of those odd moments I felt so often that season at the ranch. It was a feeling of being surrounded by things primitive and mysterious, a sense that there was a separate reality in the remote valley and that almost anything was probable.

When the arguing about tigers had lost its energy, Mamma Grande looked around, frowning. "Eighty-nine quadrillion gol-darns," she said. "You all have jawed at me so long I've lost the thread of my tale."

She talked then of Thomas Cowan, how he and another man had been captured by bandits, held prisoner in an old boxcar and told they would be shot in the morning. During the night they pried boards loose and escaped on foot through the mountains.

Was the bandit leader the famous Monty Michael, the American whose gang had terrorized eastern Mexico?

CHAPTER TEN

She didn't know.

Then, stories of how Thomas Cowan had become the unofficial doctor for the area, an expert at treating gunshot wounds, machete slashes, broken bones and all kinds of odd ailments. His son, Kenneth, a doctor himself in West Texas, said it was as though his father had some uncanny intuition that told him what to do, and that people walked for miles for the help of Don Tomas, bringing with them an almost superstitious faith in his powers.

Once, a young Mexican boy had appeared, part of his broken arm bone sticking out through his flesh. The boy asked Don Tomas to "fix my arm so my mother will not know I fell from the tree she told me not to climb."

Don Tomas set the broken bone and stitched up the wound.

"I assume the boy's mother noticed," Kenneth said.

There was a question from someone about another story, something to do with a doctor who early-on had been with the colony of Americans. Mamma Grande held up her hand and said, "Now you all just hush about that."

The faces in the room told me that only I and the young children did not know what had happened.

Mamma Grande sat quietly, nodding a little, looking pensive as though troubled by the changes of the years.

We blew out all the candles and everyone went off to bed, the young men and I to one of the cottages where there were sinister rustlings in the palm frond roof. The young men had told me that giant scorpions sometimes fell during the night. Snakes, too, especially the fierce "Fer de Lance" which caused the bitten person to "foam at the mouth before he died."

I lay awake in the darkness, partly because of the rustlings from above, but mostly because I was puzzled by the charm of the evening, and by my own strong response to it. What had made everyone such a participant, even I the outsider, even the children who had listened and asked questions, their new playthings forgotten? Was it Christmas that had helped it happen? Would the same feel of closeness have been there if that group had been gathered at Ranch Don Tomas in summer?

I didn't know. I only knew that if what my anthropology books told me was true—that storytelling was an age-old and essential ritual of passing values from generation to generation—then every family needed a wise, old storyteller like Mamma Grande.

Nothing fell on me during the night, though a large, black scorpion was on display for my benefit next morning. At the ranch house I found Mamma Grande and Jacqueline working together, gathering things for picnic lunches. "It is a day for staying in touch," Mamma Grande announced. That meant traveling by jeep and car to call on the few remaining people of the original colony.

CHAPTER TEN

She cradled a basket on her lap as we set out. In it were jars of jam (was it quince or guava?), and it reminded me of how I had long ago delivered Christmas cookies to the neighbors.

I recall our finding only three families, but there were side excursions, some of them demanded by the children. We bounced across the palmlog bridge where the baby had been rescued, everyone hanging on tight. We stopped at the cave of the Gentlemen Bandits and walked into the cool entrance. The passage to the main cavern was blocked by tons of debris that had fallen during an earthquake. Naturally, it was that hidden area which contained the treasure. Mamma Grande looked for and could not find the great clay pots she said had been there, "tall as a man."

She said the Mexican government had once sent soldiers who worked for months trying to find the silver. Evidence for that expedition was there, a tunnel leading a long way into the mountainside, ending uselessly in a face of solid stone.

Near the river, we stopped at a series of little mounds, topped with a decaying layer of limestone mortar. In the plowed field around them were fragments of ancient pottery, bits of obsidian and the flat stones and roller stones used for grinding corn.

Someone picked up a pottery head, the decorative top portion of what might have been a water jug. The forehead was slanted, a confirmation perhaps of what I had been told—that this valley was once home for a little-studied people who had links with the ancient Myan culture, hundreds of miles to the south.

I said that to the group. The skeptical young man had doubts. I was beginning to see his problem. He wanted everything to be provable, make logical sense, and he had entered a world where—as is true of Christmas—logic does not always rule.

We left the river and climbed into high country where scattered oak trees and open meadows gave a feel of African savanna. There we found the ranch of Rob and Alba Blagg, their stone house cool and dark. Mamma Grande delivered her jam and she and Alba talked of earlier days. Rob took the children outside and solemnly offered them the fiercely sour fruits that looked like tangerines. He offered me one, too. Wise now, we laughed and said no. Rob gave each child a Mexican coin and told them to put it in their pocket.

"Now," he said, "do you know what's wrong with just having one coin in your pocket?"

The children shook their heads.

"Why, with just one coin there's no jingle." He gave them each another coin and asked them to jingle for him.

We came down from the high country and found the Speedys. David Speedy seemed old and frail. When I asked about an abandoned automobile that was rusting away nearby, he remembered it as being one of the first in the area, but could not remember what kind it had been. That bothered him and he looked it over, searching in vain for a name plate. The Speedys and Mamma Grande talked on and on, trying to account for all the people who had been young when they came to Mexico.

A sidetrip on a "road" that was just two car tracks

brought us to an isolated outpost that reminded me of a Joseph Conrad story. I remember only the man, Dallas Blagg—somber, rather silent and craggy-faced, a feel of secrecy about him that made him very different from his brother Rob.

A stream ran down the mountain near the house. He had built a little waterwheel to generate electricity. Someone asked him about the pre-Columbian mounds. "They're out there," he said, pointing to the jungle-like woods of the lower country, and it was not clear to me whether he meant the mounds or the ancient people.

Mamma Grande, cradling a now-empty basket, was silent on our return trip. She seemed tired and went off to rest when we reached the ranch. A little later, I found Jacqueline sitting alone by the river. She told me the place was where people swam during warmer weather and that sometimes there really were small alligators in the river. And that there were also little fish that nuzzled swimmers legs and sent children thrashing out of the water, yelling "Alligator! Alligator!"

Downstream a little way, a crow-sized bird was screaming its name over and over—"*Chachalaca! Chachalaca!*" A pigmy kingfisher, small enough to be an ornament, posed motionless on a limb.

Jacqueline looked troubled. I sat down by her and asked what was wrong.

"She's getting old," Jacqueline said. "She's seventy-two. One day she won't be here. Then it will all be gone."

I already knew Jacqueline well enough to realize she did not like change or things unpredictable.

There had been too many unpredictables in her younger life. Her father had died when she was two months old. Her mother, Mamma Grande's oldest daughter, seemed never to have fully recovered from that death. There had been lonely, drifting times.

"It's Mamma Grande who holds it all together," Jacqueline said. "There's no one else who'll know how to make it be Christmas."

I thought of all the times during the last few days I had seen the two of them, grandmother and granddaughter, working closely together. I put my arm around Jacqueline's shoulders. "Yes there is," I said. "You will know how to make it happen."

Travels
of a Star

Jacqueline and I were married the spring after that Christmas at Rancho Don Tomas and she brought her strong feel for holiday rituals into my life. I identify her more with the Christmas season than with any other part of our life together. Christmas was one of her ways of keeping hold of her past. We soon left Mexico, the country and culture she had been born into, and, although Jacqueline lived in the United States for thirty-five years, she always meant Mexico when she used the word *home*. It reminded me of my father, though for him the words were "in the Old Country." I think we born-here Americans know little about what it is like to live out one's life with memories and emotions claimed by two countries.

It has been a surprise to me to discover that most of my own memories of Christmas are not of big family gatherings or great spreads of presents. More often memory is triggered by something small. Right now I hold in my mind the image of a star. It is the Christmas when our first child, Suzanne, is five months old. We are sitting at the kitchen table, Jacqueline all glowing and alive with the season and the knowledge of a child of our own, and we are having a contest to see who can create a perfect, five-pointed star. Having failed to find the paper-cutting instructions, we are working by trial and error, folding a sheet of paper just so, cutting with scissors, then unfolding to reveal lopsided, hopeless stars that send us into constant laughter. Nicely symmetric six-point stars we can do. Five-point stars resist us. Finally we try a more basic approach—drawing a star free-hand and cutting it out. Using that as a pattern, we cut a star from stiff cardboard, cover it with foil, edge it with tinsel, glue bits of glitter on the foil and fasten the star to the top of our Christmas tree with a straight pin. Then, close together in our own place, carols playing softly because Suzanne is now asleep, we stand and look at the lights being reflected back to us from the star.

That star, wrapped in tissue paper and seeming impervious to time, was carried from home to home and became part of every Christmas. Now, forty years later, it shines back from grown-up Suzanne's Christmas tree.

My strongest memories of our Christmases together center on the many years we lived in the country, forty miles north of New York City. Our home was a pre-Revolutionary place of beamed ceilings large fireplaces and a ten-foot square chimney going up through the middle. The house had a personality of its own. During two and a half centuries it had adjusted itself to the terrain. The children claimed they could drop a marble at the north end, and, with a little guidance at doorways, the marble would roll all the way to the south end, more than fifty feet away.

The house was a place of legends. We were told it had been a stop on the Underground Railroad for escaped slaves who were pursued by bounty hunters as they fled toward Canada. It had been an inn once for travelers on the New York–Boston stage coach route. Digging in the garden turned up a harvest of the past—oxen shoes, old bottles, pieces of English Ironstone dishes, and once, half of an old sleigh bell. While digging in that same garden four years later, I found the other half of the bell. And there were discarded, stubby-stemmed clay tobacco pipes, the kind that were rented out to travelers for the night. When a pipe was returned, a bit of the stem was broken off to "sanitize it" for the next user.

Not far from the house was a marsh, labeled on maps from the 1700s "The Musterious Vineyard." Some people liked to believe the large grapes that grew there had been brought by Vikings, and that the massive stone walls of our root cellar were the work of Druids.

Fireplace chimneys murmured and loose shakes hummed in a deep voice outside my study. The oak beams moved and spoke as the house warmed in the sun and cooled with darkness. Heating pipes expanded and contracted, rubbing against wood, making echoing noises of someone walking. The children made a friendly ghost of that sound, a peg-legged man named Mr. McGillicuddy who wandered the house looking for his daughter.

With its feel of earlier times and perhaps twenty generations of people come and gone, that house was a perfect setting for Christmas, which always borrows from the past. Houses come alive at Christmas. We went through the season feeling that someone was looking over our shoulders, nodding approval.

I am not sure those invisible people would have approved of the activity we called "Finding the Christmas Tree." It waited until the day of Christmas Eve. I don't remember why. Perhaps it started on a year when money was short and we knew trees would be cheaper then. However it began, it became an every-year ritual, proving that rituals do not necessarily depend on memory of their origin.

The search involved the three children and me, indicating, I think, that Jacqueline had better sense than I did. She waved us on our way and stayed happily behind, the kitchen table covered with mixing bowls, one for each kind of cookie she would make. With the bowls was the ancient seal, perhaps once used for decorating pottery, that I had found at the ranch in Mexico. It was used now for stamping a design on Jacqueline's "pre-Columbian shortbread."

Searching for a tree with Suzanne, Roger and Kristine meant dealing with three fiercely-held opinions. It was not just a Christmas tree they wanted. Each had some hidden inner vision of the perfect icon.

Could they tell me what they had in mind?

No. They would know it when they saw it.

No clues at all?

No. It was not possible to explain it verbally. "It's a feeling-level thing, Daddy."

That would be Suzanne, who had started speaking complicated sentences at ten months and may have been about eight years old when she was born.

Kristine, the youngest, seemed to be looking for something only half-remembered. I would find her staring wistfully at a small, neglected tree that had not won a second glance from the others. I always wondered if it had some connection with the Christmas story about the lonely doll in the store window, appealing in a quiet way that went unappreciated by all who walked by.

Roger, boxed in by age between two sisters, had territory to protect. He had once had an absolute fit when he ran into the truth that, no matter how he grew, Suzanne would always be older. He was less emotionally involved in our search, or at least pretended to be, his demand centering on a more mechanistic vision of the perfect tree. Suzanne, who sometimes has the ability to look over my shoulder even when she is a thousand miles away, would probably say "Roger just enjoys being oppositional."

Maybe that runs in the family. Suzanne now has an "oppositional" child.

My own questions about the tree were practical. Were the branches stiff enough to support the candles? Did the tree taper enough so that the lower candle flames would not be dangerously close to the next higher whorl of limbs? And, since getting the tree this late means they have all been picked over, could we maybe lower our standards a little?

No, of course not. And anyway, "You know we never buy one at the first places we look."

Questions. Arguments. Discussion. Did the tree have to be perfect even on the side that would be turned to the wall? Was it full enough? Was it bright green? Were the needles too prickly? Did we like the man or woman who was selling the trees, or did they have "an attitude?"

How does one pursue this mixture of obscure visions and practical demands? Simple. You expose all four people to as many trees as possible and maybe the perfect one will reach out and say "Here I am!"

That meant driving all over northern Westchester County, then into Putnam and Duchess counties to all the places selling trees, and then back again to look at trees already seen that were almost perfect, then back to compare those with ones more newly seen, and questions like "How come we never look for trees in Connecticut?"

"Or maybe New Jersey. Or Rockland County, on the other side of the Hudson River." That was Roger who was born loving maps, travel and automobiles.

More discussions and chaos, Kristine wondering more frequently if it was time yet to stop for hot chocolate. Sometimes those were code words for "My feet are cold," something no youngest child ever feels free to admit to older siblings.

Was this why Jacqueline stayed at home? To avoid the chaos?

No, I decided, it was something else. Hands busy, mind free to travel, she would be remembering holiday seasons in Mexico, and Mamma Grande who had died in 1965, and perhaps wondering about her mother who lived alone in Mexico City and surfaced once a year with a five-word Christmas telegram.

I kept track once of our Christmas tree journey. Without ever being more than twenty miles from home, we traveled almost a hundred. On that year, the weather changed. Heavy snow began falling, great flakes coming straight down, quieting the world. That, and other unadmitted cold feet, hastened a compromise. We made our choice and slithered and slid our way home, the tree sticking out the back of the station wagon, getting a coating of wet snow.

The ground was white at home. The dog barked at the tree, wanting to anoint it. We tugged it inside, melting snow decorating the needles with shining beads of water. The smell of pitch joined the smell of just-out-of-the-oven cookies and banana bread, a blend that said Christmas.

Intelligent Jacqueline stayed in the kitchen while new discussions began in the living room. Did the tree have to be in the same place every year? Did we have to cut it off at the bottom or was it all right for the star to stick up between two beams and touch the ceiling? Was the tree straight or did I have to put more wooden wedges under one side?

When there was agreement that the tree was straight, of course it had to be turned and become crooked again because another side might look better facing into the room.

I took out the wedges and turned the tree. "Like

this?"

"No, I meant turn it the other way."

I turned it the other way and started putting in wedges again.

"Wait. I think it was better the way it was before."

So, out with the wedges. Turn the tree. Put the wedges in.

The tree relaxed in the warmth from the fireplace, the limbs lowering a little. The decorating drops of water dried. We stepped back and admired the tree, each of us finding some different completion of a vision. I looked up and Jacqueline was standing in the living room doorway, hands clasped together above her apron, looking like a delighted child.

The decorations were already out, Jacqueline sat on the sofa, putting the little wire hangers on ornaments and handing them, one by one, for us to hang on the tree. Like Mamma Grande and like my mother, she held certain ornaments longer in her hands, seeming reluctant to let them go.

The cat appeared, made a wild run into an empty ornament box and slid with it across the floor. She was chased away but came slinking back, batted a low-hanging glass ball from the tree and pursued it along the wall. She was chased away again. The dog, still sniffing the bottom of the tree in an interested way, was put outside.

The tinseled ropes were draped in spirals around the tree. A bird's nest with an imitation oriole was placed in a whorl of limbs. Then, the candles in their special holders that gripped onto the branches. Last of all, the star at the top.

Under the tree, cradled in Spanish moss, was a crèche of Mexican pottery figures, depicting the Christmas story.

Once, a tiny spaceman appeared in the crèche, replacing baby Jesus. Who but Roger would have done that. "They might not like it," I told him.

"Who?" Roger asked.

"All the people who lived here once. Even Mr. McGillicuddy for that matter."

With Kristine or Suzanne that might have meant the spaceman would have gone back into orbit. Not so with Roger. Borrowing a phrase used often by Jacqueline, who had borrowed it from Mamma Grande, Roger dismissed the people who had gone before us. "It will be good for their character."

Decorating activity spread through the house. Every window had its figure, or bell, or snowflake. A string of brass bells was hung on the outside door. A rope for Christmas stockings was strung below the mantle of the living room fireplace.

Snow was falling and darkness came early. I lighted the kerosene lamp with its concave mercury reflector and turned the lamp and tilted the reflector to focus a bright circle of light on the treetop star.

Now a maniacal scene appears. As though there was some need to maximize confusion, all the present wrapping was done on Christmas Eve. The children took over the upstairs landing which was soon knee-deep in presents, wrapping paper and spools of ribbons that kept uncoiling even when no one was touching them.

We could hear the chaos. "Where are the scissors?

What did you do with the double-stick tape? Who took the labels?" and then the sound of someone thrashing through the wrapping paper in search. The cry, "Get out of here!" meant the cat had joined them.

Kristine once decided to wrap all her presents and put the labels on after. By then she had forgotten which was which and had to unwrap most of them.

Roger liked to disguise his gifts. A phonograph record for Suzanne could not just be wrapped. That was too obvious. When he finished, he had hidden it inside a mannequin of a private investigator, using pillows, my old London Fog trench coat and my fishing hat pulled down over a plastic bowl with a face painted on it.

Suzanne was the neatest, less a captive of the chaos. She carefully guarded her own scissors. She was suspected of hoarding all the plastic bows that had never been used before, yet was delighted with colored tissue paper that had been left near an open window and was patterned by the rain.

Despite the disaster area left behind on the landing, beautifully wrapped presents emerged and were carried down to be placed under the tree. Then we gathered in the living room and Jacqueline served cranberry juice, because it was a Christmas color, and banana bread that had been buttered and then placed for a few minutes under the broiler.

Carols were playing. An ancient wind-up music box, which had a turning wooden tree with holders for tiny candles, played Silent Night and every few bars turned itself off with a loud click. The candles on the Christmas tree were lighted. I watched them carefully as my father had watched, though there was progress. He had stood with a bucket of water, just in case. I had placed a fire extinguisher at the end of the sofa.

A small glass of cranberry juice and a cookie were put on the hearth for Santa. Stockings were hung. The music box clicked a last time. Taking turns with a candle snuffer, we put out the candles on the tree, the wicks holding pinpoints of light for a moment, then winked out and sent little spirals of smoke up toward the star and the light from the kerosene lamp.

Then to bed, the children only of course. Much was left to be done. Through some continuing insanity, there was always at least one toy that had to be assembled. Once it was an Irish Mail pedal car for Roger with instructions that might have made more sense to someone building a dirigible. Holes in the metal tubing did not match with other holes and there was noisy improvising with an electric drill. Always, at least one nut or bolt was missing. Or had the cat taken it? She liked things that clattered and would carry small objects to the top of the stairs and push them down, step by step.

Jacqueline and I still had present wrapping to do, first making certain all doors to children's rooms were closed. Next, restore the landing to order. As we picked up and smoothed out wrapping paper, the lost scissors, tapes, ribbons and bows came back to the surface. Once, we found the missing labels in the refrigerator.

Finally, to bed, then up again to go down and drink part of Santa's juice and take a bite from his cookie. We forgot it one year. The juice was untouched but a mouse had remembered to nibble the cookie.

The rest is like looking into a kaleidoscope of memory again, morning always coming too early for parents who had been assembling toys and wrapping things at two a.m. The sky lightened and from the children's rooms came loud, time-to-get-up noises that were supposed to sound accidental.

"Stay upstairs," we yelled, and went down to launch the day. I started a fire in the living room fireplace and lighted the candles in three old Mexican branding irons that stood on the mantle. The door to the living room was kept closed, the children on the stairs now, edging down step by step, the dog sitting with them, barking.

Jacqueline came from the kitchen, carrying a tray with banana bread and hot cocoa. We lighted the Christmas tree candles and the lamp with the reflector. I put "Joy to the World" on the record player, opened the living room door and that was the signal for a rush down the stairs. The rush stopped just inside the living room door. The children stood there for a moment, staring around the room that was lighted only by the candles, the fireplace and the small kerosene lamp, as though wanting to preserve that collective image of Christmas morning.

Santa Claus presents, not wrapped because that was another tradition, were in plain sight, but the children carefully did not see them right away. They went first to the bulging stockings, pulling out red Delicious apples, nuts, candies, little gifts such as whistles and nerve-shattering clickers, and sometimes magical chocolate oranges that were encased in foil, each section neatly separable.

Eyes had been turning toward the Santa presents and now they went to them and vanished from the group for a time while exploring the one present that had seemed most important in pre-Christmas discussions.

I sat on the floor by the tree, handing out presents one by one, youngest child first. Everyone else watched and waited for the unveiling and the response. Often, the gift was passed around for others to hold and see.

Then, the next present.

That meant the gift-giving lasted a great part of Christmas day, the living room slowly acquiring a carpet of crumpled wrappings which could not be picked up because the cat so enjoyed running at and burying herself in the paper.

In memory it seems it was always the same rambunctious cat, yet we lived for twenty years in that house, so it was really a sequence of cats. Why then did they behave so identically? The answer would seem to be that cats, like people, have common behaviors and rituals. None of the cats could resist small, moving toys. I remember the year Roger was given an electric train, the kind with tiny engine and cars that were hard to put onto the track. Roger would get it all set up, start it moving, and the cat, who had been lurking under a chair, would pounce, send engine and cars flying, then go back under the chair and wait for next time.

Many presents remained under the tree when it was time to become serious about Christmas dinner. The turkey had been in the oven for hours, its aroma filling the house. Everyone left presents behind and helped—building a fire in the dining room fireplace, setting the table, lighting candles, carrying steaming dishes to the table.

Dinner was a time for tale-telling, children remembering other Christmases, such as the one when a neighbor boy came by to wish us Merry Christmas, ate a full dinner with us, then excused himself saying he had to get home for Christmas dinner.

There were questions for Jacqueline and me about our earlier Christmases. Her accounts of the long Mexican holiday season—posadas, fiestas, piñata breaking, and fireworks—made my own Wisconsin Christmases seem pale.

After dinner, we went back into the living room to "do the rest of the presents." When the last one was handed out, the tempo of the day changed. Roger was using the coils of the braided rug as an unending road for his Lesney cars. Suzanne was smoothing out delicately patterned candy wrappers to put into the encyclopedia with the flowers put there in summer. The tired cat was wearing a tiny sun bonnet and being wheeled around by Kristine in a doll carriage.

Then, excursions out into the winter—sleds to be tried on the symmetrical knoll we called Indian Hill, snowballs to be thrown, cookies to be taken across the road to the Coe's, a sheaf of grain for the birds, and refilling of the squirrel-proof bird feeder that had been emptied by the squirrels.

On our way back inside, hands cold from rolling pillars of wet snow for a snowman, we stopped at the porch to gather up wood. The lowering western sun was illuminating bittersweet berries encased in icicles that hung from the eaves. The bittersweet vines had spiraled up the metal downspout, half crushing it, and were climbing upward toward the rooftop.

It was Kristine who noticed how the vines were all spiraling in the same direction.

"Vines always do that," I said.

"Why?"

"It has something to do with the rotation of the Earth."

I think Roger was being only partly oppositional when he objected. "Vines don't always do that," he said. "South of the equator they grow around things in the opposite direction."

Suzanne had a little smile that said she knew he was going to say that.

"Absolutely right," I said, hoping she would realize it was for her, too.

Each child picked up an armload of wood and went inside. I watched the three of them go. I looked again at the bittersweet vines, and I marveled at the wonder of children, nature and life in general.

There was change.

Decorating the tree and all the other activities of Christmas Eve had become a long established part of Christmas. One year, the children were not part of that. They were older now and had all gone off to Christmas activities of their own.

Jacqueline did not like change, especially the kind that threatened family rituals. She was silent as the two of us worked on the tree and decorated the house. At some point, I realized she was quietly crying as she worked, the change bringing to light old ghosts of childhood losses and loneliness.

I tried to comfort her. She shook her head and went on with the decorating. When the children came bursting back from their enlarging worlds, she became herself again. The house took on its normal Christmas energy. I don't think the children ever knew how strongly she reacted to that foretaste of inevitable change.

After twenty Christmases in the New York house, the children gone to their own lives, Jacqueline and I left it behind and moved to my old home in Wisconsin. It was change again. Jacqueline came to the "Middle West," saying she was leaving in the East her children, her house, her teaching and her health.

We all gathered one last time for Christmas. The old decorations had come with us and filled the farmhouse. The lamp with the mercury reflector hung in the living room and illuminated the same star at the top of the tree, but the house was quiet. Jacqueline was on oxygen now for her emphysema. At Christmas dinner she looked around the table, frowning as though something was missing. We waited, knowing a pronouncement was coming.

"Christmas is not Christmas without children," she said. She looked almost accusingly at Suzanne and Kristine and said, "This house needs grandchildren. You two are wasting the talents of two perfectly good grandparents."

There was silence around the table. Roger was smiling, probably wondering why he was excused from the duty of grandchildren. Logs shifted in the fireplace. Sparks rose, the kind that fly out and then explode in the air with a little flash and snap.

Suzanne was pregnant with grandchild Sarah

Margaret by the next spring. Jacqueline knew about that before her death in the middle of July.

We gathered in Wilmington, Delaware at Suzanne's house for the next Christmas. The star Jacqueline and I had made, the year Suzanne was born, was at the top of her Christmas tree.

The Year We Didn't Have a Christmas Tree

I have come to a pause, knowing I've wandered far from early Christmases. Something is telling me to let this search do what I have done myself, come home again, to this land, to the house where I was born, to my childhood memories of our days together as a family.

I watch the wind-whipped green of a white pine tree in the yard and am reminded of the year we didn't have a Christmas tree. It is a story I have told before, but that time, perhaps more than any other, speaks to me about all the feelings and the wonder that live in the word "Christmas."

The season began as usual. The last day of school came, and that was the first day of Christmas for us. Teacher as always on the day, had a frantic look. We could not stay in our seats or keep from whispering.

"Let's meet! Let's go sledding!"

"When?"

"Tomorrow! Day after tomorrow! Next week!"

"Let's each say we're going to stay at the other's house. We'll dig a snow cave. We'll sled all night."

"If there's a wet snow, let's all come back to school. Let's start a big snowball. Let's roll it down the hill until it's big as the schoolhouse."

"Yeah, and maybe knock the schoolhouse down!"

We squirmed in our seats, and we weren't even there. We were racing down the hills on our sleds, snow flying up to pelt us, giving us faces so white that only our eyes showed through and surely the adults would faint and scream when they saw us, thinking we were ghosts.

All Teacher could think of was the school program that night. We were her performers, and we couldn't even remember our own names.

"Quiet. Get back to your seats. Stop that whispering."

We stayed an extra half-hour to practice the singing. Teacher couldn't seem to get us all to use the same words. For "Jingle Bells" was it "Bells on bob tail ring," or was it "Bells on bob-tailed Ned" (or "Nag" or "Nob")?

"You've got me so confused I don't remember myself," Teacher said. "Let's agree it's Ned."

We tried another song. "No! No! It's 'We Three Kings of Orient Are', not 'We Three Kings of Oriental.' And when you're singing 'Silent Night,' remember that it's 'round yon virgin,' not 'round, young virgin.'"

"Can you all remember that?"

"Yes," we cried, the feel of our sled ropes already in our hands. We would have said yes if she'd asked if we each had thirty-nine heads.

A first-grade girl had to stay after school for more work with Teacher. She had decided to recite the Lord's Prayer and she kept saying, "Our Father Who are in Heaven, Halloween be Thy name."

We ran for home, pulling our sleds, still making plans.

"Let's build a ski jump!"

"Let's pour water all over the hillside west of the house and slide on the frozen crust."

We had used water once to make an icy crust on the big snowdrift between the house and barn. Father and Lyle didn't know about that. They started across the drift carrying a ten-gallon can full of milk. It was a good crust all right. After Father and Lyle fell down, they stayed on top and slid all the way down to the chicken house. When the milk can caught up with them, it still had enough in it to slosh them good. Father suggested we not do that any more. He also suggested we spend the next day shoveling a path through the big snowdrift.

But a whole hillside of ice would be different! We'd go flying down toward the fence, skim under the lower strand of barbed wire, teeter on the edge of the ditch, and go all the way to the woods!

Junior wasn't there to ask things like how would we get the water out there and what if we hit a bump just as we went under the barbed wire. He was at home with a cough. When we came crashing into the kitchen, Father and Mother were talking about whether or not Junior should go to the school program that night. Junior was looking from one to the other as they talked, his face pale, eyes very big. He smiled when they decided it would be all right.

We did the chores before supper. Lyle finished the last of his hot coffee in one noisy gulp and hurried out to get the horses and the big bobsled ready. With the yellow light of a lantern to show us the way, we went out to the sled. Lyle had filled the two-foot-high sled box with straw and put all our old blankets on top. Mother had heated several of her irons on top of the kitchen stove and brought them along, wrapped in old towels, in case anyone's feet got cold.

We blew out the lantern and climbed in, pulling blankets around us. Lyle was up front. He flipped the lines, said "Gid-y-ep," and we glided out along the ridge to the west, the wind reaching for us, tug chains ringing like bells behind the trotting horse.

Our eyes adjusted to the darkness. A faint blue light seemed to hang just over the surface of the snow. We could see the graceful roll of the drifts along the road, the smooth outline of snow-covered fields, the faint shadow of the next ridge to the north and beyond that the lights of Mount Sterling.

Father was wearing his old horsehair coat and had promised he would leave it in the sled. Mother's hands were tucked deep into her big fur muff, holding it up to protect her face from the wind. Junior was huddled almost out of sight in Father's big sheepskin coat. The sled runners rattled sometimes when we hit crusted snow.

"Look!" Mother said, pointing.

There were glittering little pinpoints of light shining in a field where the wind had swept away the snow and uncovered patches of smooth ice.

"What are they?"

"The reflections of the stars," said Father.

We lay down on our backs, protected from the wind, sinking deep into the straw with its smell of summer, and we looked up at the distant stars.

"How many do you think there are?"

"A billion, I bet."

"A trillion."

"Ten thousand quadrillion."

"So many you could spend the rest of your life counting them and still not count them all."

"Is it always the same stars?"

"Of course it is."

"I mean if you tried to count them, would they all just stay there and be the same ones?"

"Hey, maybe there's stars that just visit us, maybe once every thousand years."

"Comets do that, not stars."

"Well, why shouldn't a star be able to do that if a comet can?"

"Shush," said Mother. "Just enjoy them."

We went on into the shelter of the woods. The wind was almost gone, the breath of the horses quick and white as they walked up the steep hill beyond the deep ravine. We topped the hill and turned down into the narrow school road, sled runners sliding silently through the undisturbed snow, bare limbs of trees so thick above us they almost shut out the stars. An owl hooted. Something quick and small, a rabbit maybe, scurried away from the road and vanished in the woods.

"There's the light," Lyle said as we came down into the little hollow that led to the schoolhouse. The runners of other sleds were rattling on the icy road beyond the creek. Horses were whinnying. Yellow lights bobbed up and down in the meadow east of the schoolhouse where people were coming on foot, carrying kerosene lanterns. We found a place between two other teams, tied up to the top rail of the fence, and Father and Lyle covered the horses with blankets.

The schoolhouse was warm, filled with the light and smell of a half-dozen kerosene lamps. One was flickering. Mother smiled at me. "It needs you to trim the wick."

The big wreath we had made from pine limbs and bittersweet berries was hanging under the clock. The blackboard had hundreds of dabs of chalk on it.

"I told you it wouldn't look like snow," Junior said when he saw the blackboard. His voice was a hoarse whisper. He stayed with Mother in a front seat, his hands tucked inside her muff. Soon the room was crowded, some people dressed "in their best bib and tucker," as Mother would say, some in work clothes that carried a barn smell through the warm room. There was a burst of laughter when a long-legged man tried to squeeze into the desk he'd used when he was in the eighth grade.

"Look," he said pointing at the desk top, "there's my initials."

Several high-school boys stood at the back of the room, whispering and laughing. A girl near them got up, marched to the front, and crowded into another seat, her face as red as the ribbon in her hair.

Teacher welcomed everyone. Mostly she talked about how hard we had worked. I think she was asking people not to laugh at our mistakes.

We all trooped out of the cloakroom for our first number, jostled into position, and sang "Jingle Bells," almost everyone remembering to say "Bells on bob-tailed Ned."

The next number was "Scenes from an Early Wisconsin Christmas." The piano began. An Indian crept out, an arrow ready in his half-drawn bow. When his head feather slipped he grabbed for it and the arrow went up in the air and came down on the piano keyboard, playing one sharp pinging note. The woman at the piano, I think her name was Elsie, slid over to the other end of the bench. It tipped and dumped her off. She reached up and went right on playing while she was getting up from the floor.

Tom Withers came in, crawling on all fours, playing a hungry bear. The Indian was supposed to shoot him, but he couldn't find his arrow. Tom ran in circles, one of them bringing him close to the Christmas tree. His head went through a loop in a string of popcorn. Tom kept on going. The tree tipped and came down on top of him. He roared, as a bear or as himself we never knew, and galloped off with the string of popcorn following.

The audience did its best. People were able to control their laughter until a boy came out for the first lines of our scene.

"Christmas in early Wisconsin," he said, "was not an easy time."

"By God, you can say that again," boomed a voice from the back. "What with bears in the house and all."

The room filled with laughter. Men were pounding their legs and wiping tears out of their eyes. The women stopped first and began shushing everyone until it was quiet again.

A third-grader marched out to do her piece about Christmas fairies. After four sentences or so, she forgot her lines and switched over and did "The Village Blacksmith" instead. The audience applauded anyway and she walked off, head high, looking very pleased.

A boy did part of "Snowbound." I don't think he understood the opening lines because he always put a question mark after them. "The sun that cold December day, it sank from sight before it set?"

A girl began reciting "The First Snowfall." Halfway through, her little brother wandered up front and stood looking at her. She went on speaking, shooing him away with her hands, but he stayed right beside her. She stopped for a minute, sighed, then took his hand and went on with the poem, the little boy beaming at her. There was a line in that poem about someone kissing a child, then lines something like "And she kissing back could not know that the kiss was meant for her sister, lying deep under the falling snow."

The girl took the little boy back to his seat and walked to the cloakroom. The audience was very quiet, except that one old lady in a white shawl was crying. Then the applause came, longer for that girl than for any other part of the program.

We all lined up and started singing "Joy to the World," but were interrupted by the sound of horses fighting. Half the men ran outside, and we waited, frozen in the middle of a line, until everyone came back. The piano started again at the beginning. We went on from where we were. At the end, an angel was supposed to walk across in front of us. One of her wings fell off. She tripped on it and said, in a clear whisper, "Darn! I told her it wouldn't stay on."

Everything else went all right unless you counted a key sticking on the piano and a man prying it up with his jackknife.

At the end, we all jostled into line again and sang "Silent Night." I don't think we said the virgin was round. The old lady started crying again. Teacher walked out in front of us and said, "Everybody sing!"

The schoolhouse rumbled and vibrated as all the voices joined in.

We waited for the applause to end, bowed and started to walk off, but there was a cold blast of air from the door and Santa Claus bounced in with a big bag on his shoulder. He went "ho-ho-ing" around the room, stopping every few steps to pull up his slipping belly, asking who had been good all year in a voice suspiciously like that of one of our closest neighbors,

Amel Oppriecht. He came up to the front, reached into his bag, and handed each of us a little brown paper sack full of hard candy, peanuts and a big sticky popcorn ball that stuck in the top of the sack like a bottle stopper.

Santa went all around the room with little sacks for the younger children and for Junior, pretending each time that his bag was empty. Then he bounced back out the door. We could hear him yelling out in the schoolyard. "Gid-y-ep, Dancer! Gid-y-ep, Prancer!"

We crowded to the windows. He was riding off in a sled. Bells were ringing, and he yelled, "Merry Christmas to all, and to all a goodnight!"

The sled, the voice and the bells faded slowly into the night.

The piano started up again. Everyone crowded around to sing carols, and the smell of the kerosene stove filled the room as women began making coffee and hot cocoa. Soon it was ready, great steaming pots of both, along with about a hundred different kinds of cookies that were shaped like stars, trees and bells, most of them covered with bright-colored sugar.

Warm, and so full of cocoa we could hear it sloshing when we wiggled our stomachs, we started home. Lanterns were going in all directions, the night filled with young and old voices.

"Merry Christmas!"

"Goodnight. Merry Christmas."

"See you in two weeks."

"Don't forget we're going to roll a big snowball."

We went up the road, Denny Meagher and his sister, Margaret, close behind us in their sled. We said "Goodnight" and "Merry Christmas" to them, then turned out along Seldom Seen ridge by ourselves. The moon had come up. The trees made sharp black shadows on the snow. Mother began singing "Oh, Little Town of Bethlehem," her voice high and clear, getting lost out against the bright stars. Father's deep voice joined her, his Norwegian accent more noticeable when he was singing. We all sang, except Junior, as the horses trotted toward home.

We got out in front of the house and Lyle took the horses on to the barn. Junior was coughing, looking very white when Father carried him inside.

"Open the davenport," Mother said to Lee and me.

The davenport was in the living room. We opened it and Father put Junior down, then carried coals from the dining room stove for a fire. Sticky from the popcorn balls and still working on the hard candy and peanuts, we went off to bed with two weeks of vacation ahead and plans enough to fill a year.

Junior was still sick the next day and the day after that. The door to the living room stayed closed except when we tiptoed in to put more wood in the stove.

Dr. Farrell came from Seneca, bundled up in a big fur coat and cap, looking like a bear in his little sleigh that we called a cutter. We ran out to take his horse.

"I'll give her some water and oats," Lyle said.

"You will, will you?" Dr. Farrell roared. He had a voice, Lyle liked to say, that was like a cream can full of walnuts rolling down a steep hill. The doctor headed for the house with his bag, then yelled over his shoulder, "By God, it's a help all right, having the horse taken care of."

We watched from the dining room doorway while he warmed his stethoscope over the stove and listened to Junior's throat and chest. He left the thermometer in for a long time, "Cause it's cold as a damned icicle to start with!" When he read the thermometer, he came out into the dining room, closing the door behind him. Father and Mother were waiting.

"Scarlet fever," Dr. Farrell said.

"What does that mean?"

"Means he's going to be a mighty sick boy. Keep the other children out of that room. Be better if only one of you goes in there." He went on talking to Mother while we got his horse and hitched it to the cutter.

Junior kept getting worse, his fever so high we could hear him mumbling and talking in his sleep even with the door closed. Once he said in a loud, angry voice, "I said I wanted skis!"

It was a strange Christmas season. We didn't do any of the things we'd planned. Mother hardly had time to talk to us, except to tell us what needed to be done. Dr. Farrell came every day. Then, maybe four or five days before Christmas, Mother told us there wouldn't be a Christmas tree.

"We'll do something about it later, maybe. There just isn't enough time now. Anyway, the doctor says we have to keep the house quiet." She was almost crying when she went into the other room and closed the door.

"You help her all you can," Father said. "Don't wait to be asked."

"Is Junior going to get well?"

He looked at us for a long time. "We don't know," he said.

I don't remember how Laurance felt about what was happening, but Lee and I began to feel cheated. In the safe isolation of the big dark closet at the head of the stairs, we dared to come right out and tell each other there wasn't any Santa Claus. We already knew it wasn't Santa who brought our presents, but he had gone on being a part of Christmas for a long time and we still believed in Christmas, all right. But what kind of a Santa Claus, even if he was just a "spirit," would let Junior get this sick at Christmastime?

We still ran to meet the mailman every day, hoping for packages, especially packages with revealing rattles or holes in them. One day George Holliday handed us one that didn't need a hole. He winked and laughed. "Here you are. What comes in a package four inches wide, five feet long, and curves up at one end?"

"Junior's new skis," we said

"How is he?"

"Still sick."

"Well, when he gets his skis, he'll be better."

"He won't be getting them. We don't even have a Christmas tree."

"Well hell's bells," George said. "No wonder he's sick."

We took the skis to the house and gave them to Mother. She put them away. "He might not even know if I gave them to him."

Lee and I spent more and more time in the dark

closet. Other Christmases began to form in our minds as we talked. Getting boughs from the white pines for a tree, making strings of popcorn and cranberries, turning the lamps down low and watching the candles burning on Christmas Eve while we ate hard round candies with pictures in the center that were a promise of what was to come.

Christmas Day always began with the presents, handed out and unwrapped one by one. There were great bowls of nuts and candy and fruit, navel oranges and bright red apples that made our own seem pale and small.

Soon the smells of Christmas dinner would spread through the house, so strong and good we forgot our presents and gathered, starving, in the kitchen to help and hinder and hurry Mother along. Father said a blessing in Norwegian and we ate until we couldn't hold another bite, then ran around the table four times and ate some more.

After dinner, Mother would bring out the heavy package that was wrapped in brown paper. Each December she mailed a letter to the State Lending Library, asking them to send us about thirty books for three adults and four boys. She gave our ages and a few words about each of us. She'd never let us read what she said, though sometimes she included our suggestions, things like "More about cowboys and please don't send Black Beauty again this year." Then people in the library in far-off Madison would read the letter and would, we liked to think, sit down, close their eyes, see us, and decide which books to send.

Only then, with everyone gathered in the warm

house, with presents, books to read, and all the good things to eat, would Christmas have really come.

Lee and I could go back over all that in the closet, but this time it didn't happen. When we ran into the dining room on Christmas morning the day was just like any other, except that Mother looked sad and hollow-eyed and Father was walking restlessly around the room. Dr. Farrell came right after breakfast. We heard him say something about "today being a critical day."

When the doctor left, Mother brought out a present for each of us. They weren't tied with the usual bows and ribbons. I guess Father must have wrapped them. Lee and I got the double-barreled popguns we'd been wanting. Wondering how we could have missed a package that slim and long, we tore them out of the boxes, cocked them, and started to pull the double triggers. Father grabbed us.

"Better go outdoors with those."

We went out and tried target practice for a while, using twigs, corks and pieces of ice for bullets. It began to snow, big wet flakes. We rolled giant snowballs, leaving paths of bare brown lawn behind us, and made a snowman, then used our new pop-guns to shoot marbles into his front for buttons.

It didn't feel like Christmas, even with the snow falling. We sat down with our backs against the snowman and waited for something to happen.

What happened was that a man we'd never seen before came walking along the road from the west. He was wearing a stocking cap and had a stick over his shoulder with a little bundle on the end. Sometimes tramps came by with a bundle like that, heading for the railroad along the Kickapoo River. The man saw us sitting there against the snowman and waved to us.

"Merry Christmas!" he called in a big voice.

We waved back, and he went on walking down the road with the snow falling around him.

We started talking about Junior and Christmas again. The first thing we decided was that Junior should get his skis. But we had to do more than that.

"We could say Santa Claus came by with them."

That wasn't going to be good enough for skeptical Junior.

"What if somebody did come by?"

"Yeah, somebody like an old man with a stocking cap and a bundle on his back."

"What if he asked how come we're just sitting here?"

"Yeah, and we said because our brother's sick."

"And maybe he'd be like Mr. Holliday. He'd say, 'No wonder he's sick. What you need to do is take him his present.'"

"And tell him he's going to be all right."

"Do you think he'd believe that?"

"Maybe the old man better have a beard."

"Yes, a red beard."

Dr. Farrell stopped by again and we followed him into the house. He came back out of the other room and said, "He's no better."

"Can we see him?" Lee asked.

Mother shook her head.

"We want to give him his skis."

Mother looked at Dr. Farrell. He sighed. "Oh, it can't hurt anything. But don't go up close. Stay away from the bed."

Mother got the skis. We unwrapped them and took them in, closing the door behind us. Junior was lying on his back, two pillows under his head. His eyes were open but he didn't look at us. He was making a funny noise when he breathed, and his freckles stood out very plain. He didn't even seem like Junior.

We held up the skis so he could see them. We started telling him about the old man.

Pretty soon Junior looked at us. When he started shaking his head a little bit, it was Junior all right.

"Tramp" he whispered.

"No, it wasn't! He had a long beard."

"A red one!"

Junior stopped shaking his head and seemed to be thinking about that. We shoved the skis onto the bed and pushed them up beside him. He took a deep breath and closed his eyes.

We tiptoed out.

"Did you give him the skis?"

"Yes. And he went to sleep."

Mother started for the other room. Dr. Farrell stopped her. He went in and closed the door. When he came out he looked surprised. "That's right. He is asleep. I think he's breathing better."

Mother hugged us. For the first time it seemed like Christmas.

Four or five days later, when Dr. Farrell came by,

he said Junior could get up the next day. Mother smiled and said she thought maybe she'd go to bed when he got up. She looked at us. "I'm sorry about the tree."

"Hummph!" said Dr. Farrell. "Seems to me Christmas came anyway!"

Another Season

I walked again out across the fields of this farm to my thinking-place hilltop. The wind was singing its little song in the tops of trees and pushing at the tiny juniper that has had the audacity to come into life close against one of the big bur oaks.

The juniper was not the only green in the clearing. The promise of spring was there in the swelling buds, the new grass pushing up through the brown of last year's growth, the chickadees already trying out their "*pee-wee*" song.

This change of season is a contradiction. It takes time to put words down on paper in a form that pleases me. I must now say hello to spring when I have just finished recapturing lost Christmases.

What has my search told me?

I know it was a poor question I asked myself in the beginning: could I keep from mixing up the me of childhood and me of now? Of course I could not. I am both. I am every age I have ever been.

I know there is something in Christmas, fragile as the laughter of children, that wakens the sleeping goodness in us, making it easier to feel, show and say "I love you."

I know I have rediscovered lost parts of myself, as I so often do when I write, and that has told me I owe much to many people, debts I will never pay except in how I live my life.

I know that the essence hidden behind the word "Christmas" is still mysterious to me. And that this is how it should be. Leave rational explanations to the academics. Magic needs no analysis.

I have learned that each time I try to become analytical about Christmas, something else happens. There is an irresistible segue into images and feelings—lamplight reflecting from a treetop star, walking across the fields with my hand in my father's, going outside with my mother to listen to the tiny, whispering sound of falling snow.

I have learned that memory does not fool around with the trivial. It records the important, and creates its own reality. In an early story I spoke of how someone in my childhood would always say "Remember the time the dog knocked over the tree?" That happened before my time, but one year I beat everyone else and said it myself. No one realized that I only remembered through their remembering.

Perhaps that is what I have learned most of all. To keep Christmas safe from careless change and the tarnish of forgetting, I must keep remembering to remember.

Afterword

Whenever I write about events from my past, as I did in my book *The Land Remembers*, and as I've done here, I seem to set off echoes in readers as though this farm, my family and my own life have become a story. Hundreds of letters ask what time has done to the story, what are the missing pieces and the endings. Other readers make journeys to this isolated ridge, stopping at farms for directions. Neighbors send them on to me, calling them "pilgrims." That has become a kind of local joke, half serious because the pilgrims, like the letter writers, are looking for a continuing story.

Perhaps this time I can answer some of the persistent questions in advance for readers of these remembered Christmases.

I went off to college the year after Mother died. My father told me she had made him promise to make that happen if he could. "I wanted all our sons to go," she had told him. "Ben is the last chance." I had not known of the request and the promise. When the time came, Father did not ask me if I wanted to go. He told me I was going.

When I was leaving, Lyle (the hired man known to the neighbors as the oldest Logan boy) told me I was going to come back using words so long "a team of horses won't be able to pull them."

I was lucky in college. I had a driving hunger to learn that endeared me to my teachers. On my first day, I walked into the library and stood immobilized by the seemingly unending rows and rows of books. A young librarian came over to me and said, "What do you want to know?"

"Everything," I said.

She spent an hour or more showing me exactly how a library was arranged, how to use the card catalog, how to pursue any subject. From then on, each time she saw me in the library she would smile and say "What do you want to know this time?" and would help anytime I lost my way.

A geology professor read a story of mine in the college literary magazine and sought me out to talk about it. He soon became a private teacher for all my questions about the layers of fossils I found exposed in limestone cliffs along a nearby river. He gave me names for the fossils. He taught me to see

152

how each succeeding layer revealed a growing complexity of life forms. "It is a diagram of evolutionary creation," he told me.

A young biology professor became my personal guide to understanding what I was seeing in the living, natural world. I told him once that I had seen a purple gallinule along a creek and had reported it to the monthly bulletin of the Wisconsin Society of Ornithology. The editor said the sighting of such a rare bird must be questioned without a specimen record. I can still see the rueful smile of the young biology professor when I asked him what that meant.

"You were supposed to kill it," he said.

My writing quickly caught the attention of English professor Rachel Salisbury. She told me I had a special talent for touching people's feelings. No one had ever suggested that I had a talent. The word was barely in my vocabulary. In high school, when I told the principal I wanted to be a writer, he said it was too late because "all great writers start much younger." I was seventeen at the time.

Dr. Salisbury kept using the word talent. She told me that using one's talent well was a serious responsibility. She also kept nudging me in two directions at once: put more substance into my stories and, most of all, dare to be even more emotional—not an easy task for a farm boy who had grown up with the careful cliché phrases that protect rural people from seeming too emotional or too personal.

Years later, I thought of Dr. Salisbury when doing graduate work at the University of Wisconsin in Madison. Legendary English Professor Helen White, the woman who always wore purple, attempted to read one of my stories to her class and kept breaking into tears.

Those teachers so affirmed my wide-ranging curiosity that I came to believe the questions we ask often tell us more than the answers we find.

I was still part of the summer work crew on the farm. By then, Laurance and Lee had left the farm. Then Junior, who had a feeling for farming that was stronger than my own, came back from the city. There had always been a special bond between the two of us and it grew during those summers we worked together. I was still youngest son to Father. To Junior I had become an equal.

Junior died when he was twenty-four, of kidney problems almost surely linked with his scarlet fever of many years before. For a time when I thought of him, I was so unprepared for his death that I could not see his face. Later, his face returned to me, always that half-smiling combination of benevolent acceptance and skepticism.

Laurance, Lee and I, following in our sailor-father's young footsteps, were all in the Navy during WW II. I was the last to go. Father and Lyle drove me to Boscobel to catch the train which would take me to midshipman school in Chicago. Father was feeling lonesome as we waited for the train. With Junior gone, he was quite sure none of us would return to take over the farm.

Smiling a little, he turned to Lyle and said, "Lyle, I'll rent you the farm. I'll sell you the farm. No, I'll give you the farm."

Lyle, without a smile, said, "Sam, if you give me that farm, I'll sue you."

From the train window I watched the two of them walk to the car and start back to the farm where they would find an empty house. I know nothing of what kind of a Christmas they had that year, or of any of the years while all three of us were overseas, Laurance in the South Pacific, Lee in England, I in the Mediterranean.

We all returned from the war but Father had been right. We did not come back to the farm. He sold it soon after, remarried and moved to the little town of Blue River. We became very close then, a rarity I think between a rural father and son. I had gone to war still a boy in his mind. When I came back he accepted me as a man. We were adult-to-adult friends.

He died of leukemia the day after his seventy-ninth birthday. A cousin, a recent immigrant from Norway, had come to see him at the hospital the day before. The two of them spoke with each other in Norwegian, as Father had been doing more and more in his last days. The cousin told me the last thing Father had said was to remind him of an "Old Country" proverb. He translated it for me: "Man predicts, but God decides."

Laurance and Lee both live in Wisconsin, though not close-by. We are good friends but, inevitably, far removed from the closeness of children growing up together. I have learned that each child in a family has a separate childhood. When my brothers first read *The Land Remembers*, they came to me and challenged some of the events, saying I must have made them up. Then they talked of other events and asked, "Why in the world didn't you write about them?"

"I don't remember those," I said. "You must be making them up."

The cause of such confusion, I think, is that memory stores what touches us strongly on a feeling level. Feelings defy time. They can be recovered.

My own life has been busy, diverse and somewhat beyond my understanding, not so much planned as it is accidental. Life wanders by, doors open unexpectedly and I say yes and walk through them, with part of me standing back to observe my own reactions to the new worlds I find.

I wandered after the war. I had not come far enough away from it to find peace in the quiet of Wisconsin. I spent the seemingly mandatory time as a struggling writer in New York's Greenwich Village. I shipped out as a merchant seaman. I lived and studied in Mexico. I helped build bridges in Alaska. I worked as a magazine editor and film writer for Ford Motor Company, and was a film and television writer/producer for the national communications agency of the United Methodist Church. I wrote and helped produce network documentaries for NBC News. (One of them won a best program Emmy award in 1987.) And I taught creative writing, even though it has been said that "teaching has ruined more good writers than alcohol." The slurred ambiguity of that statement makes me wonder if its author had already gone the alcohol route.

During all that time, my early experiences had a way of finding their way into my conversation and writing. People sometimes asked if I regretted separating myself so far from the Wisconsin land. "There is no separation," I told them. "I am always there." I don't think they realized, and perhaps even I did not realize, how often I drew on the values of my parents and the community of my younger years. The land itself, one must understand, was a living part of that community, its own strong teacher.

With "progress" beginning to encircle that pre-Revolutionary house in New York, I returned in 1986 to the tired buildings and a hundred acres of the farm. I have been a disappointment to some people. I'm not nearly as sentimental about living in this old house as people want me to be. The idea that an important part of me has always been here, seems a difficult concept to accept.

Just how programmed I am by the past was revealed in an odd incident. (Remember, I had been away from this house for more than forty years.) During the renovation, I changed the opening to the stairway from the dining room to the living room. Yet, I one day walked out of my study to go upstairs, walked past the open stairway, went into the dining room and found myself standing before a stairway door that was no longer there.

The log walls of the 1885 part of the house are now visible on the inside. Mother's mission bookcase stands close to where it always stood. Father's favorite sailing ship picture again hangs in the bedroom. Every time I dig in the yard or garden I turn up the past—fragments of Mother's Blue Willow dishes, a broken piece of Father's workbench vise, the tongue and front axle of our old coaster wagon, the wobbly wheel from the hand-pushed garden cultivator, pieces of harness leather and hardware that remind me of favorite horses—Doll, Beauty, potbellied Flossy and fiercely-competitive Sally.

People bring me things that have strayed. Some of Mother's Jewel Tea mixing bowls have come home and recently, the ornate blue sugar bowl. The framed marriage certificate of Father and Mother's Christmas Day wedding turned up in the attic of a house in Blue River. I recently found Father's naturalization papers which, among other things, required him to renounce forever all allegiance and fidelity to any foreign entity, "particularly to Oscar II, King of Norway and Sweden."

My mother's treadle-powered Singer sewing machine is here, but searched for and missing still is the small tin box in which Father carried lily of the valley bulbs across the sea from his mother's garden.

This harvest from the past does not become somber, though there are momentary feelings of regret for something not said or questions not asked. Almost always there is a charm in these reminders, a sense of continuity. We do not lose people who have been part of us.

My children became rooted in the East during their childhood and are still there, Suzanne in Wilmington, Delaware, Kristine near New Paltz, New York. Roger is New York City-oriented and, though he likes the peace and beauty of Wisconsin, he may not be sure there is cultural validity west of the Hudson River. I think he makes an exception for me.

So, in this setting, in this familiar house, I live, I write. I sometimes teach, though with younger students, I often laugh at them and tell them, "I feel like I am teaching English as a first language."

I learn about nature from the woods and meadows and from looking out my windows, and from nature I learn about we humans. Right now outside the kitchen window a pugnacious goldfinch, tiny as it is, seems determined to keep all other birds away from the feeder. It stands on the little wooden bar, facing away from the sunflower seeds, on constant guard, pecking fiercely at all who dare come close. A cardinal lands, much larger and with a formidable bill. The goldfinch attacks. The cardinal ignores it, picks up a sunflower seed and opens it in its bill. The goldfinch tries to crowd the cardinal off, but now a titmouse lands on the other end of the perch. The goldfinch runs over to attack. The titmouse grabs one seed and leaves. A chickadee lands and the goldfinch attacks, and on and on.

My mother would almost surely have said that the goldfinch got up on the wrong side of the bed this morning. When I watch these little fables, I find myself creating moral captions, perhaps in this case: "If you spend all your time protecting territory you never get to eat." Or maybe something nicely ambiguous: "The ultimate reward for greed is starvation."

A shy ten-year-old girl who read *The Land Remembers* once asked if I talked to birds, "Of course," I said. "They talk to me, too, especially the chickadees when I bring more sunflower seeds to the feeder. I rattle the tin bucket and they fly to me and speak. It would be rude not to talk to them."

The girl began smiling, as though I had given her permission to do something she had wanted to do but did not know if it was all right.

The people who seek me out provide an interesting affirmation of my approach to writing. My goal is to make what I write the feeling-level property of the reader, each bringing his or her memories, images and emotions to my words. It seems to work. By now every chapter in The Land Remembers has been championed by someone as the best in the book. Why? Because some trigger in that chapter allowed the reader to become a personal participant and make it a part of the reader's own story.

An analogy: a painting, no matter how masterfully accomplished, is not art until a circle has been completed by people experiencing the painting and bringing something of themselves to it.

So it is with writing. I am dependent on the creativity of the reader. Writers do not make people laugh and cry. A writer supplies words that open doors to the feelings, but it is the reader who responds to those words and supplies the laughter and tears.

I began this Afterword simply to build a chronology that might help answer questions, but even that kind of writing takes unexpected turns and becomes a journey of discovery. A fragile connection is forming, telling me that more must be said about the pilgrims.

The letter writers and those who come in person are wanting to link with something. Many address me as "Ben" then acknowledge that familiarity by saying in varying ways, "You don't know me but I know you."

Some expect time to have stood still, almost wanting me to be a barefoot child still wearing bib overalls. Some are very articulate, asking progressively focused questions like a lawyer trying to reassemble an illusive reality.

Some look for icons. They want to touch the massive trunk of the big maple tree, feel the bark of the white pines from which we put together boughs for our Christmas tree. They want to know where Lost Valley is. They ask if the schoolhouse is still there and if the big pines are still in Halls Branch Valley. (It is and they are.)

Some pilgrims do not know what they are looking for. Their wistful quest seems driven by a voice playing inside them, saying "What I'm doing and who I am now can't be all there is." Their quest reminds me of two lines of poetry from *the lives and times of archie and mehitable*, by Don Marquis: "My heart has followed all my days/Something I cannot name."

On a more playful level, I am also reminded of Dylan Thomas, who for me spoke of how inexplicable life is when he said his Christmas books "told him everything about the wasp except why."

Some pilgrims are at a turning point. Weary of city tempos that leave little time for reflection, they search for ways to recover some of the lifestyle of a time when family members worked closely together and neighbors were formed into community by their need of each other.

Time magazine, in its review of *The Land Remembers*, said of such searches, "The pastoral dream is as persistent as tennis elbow." That odd combining of rural and suburban clichés has a validity. Those who try to recapture the pastoral dream too literally will be disappointed. Mechanization has made farming a more lonely way of life and has long-since ended the ritual of neighbors working together at harvest time.

Many pilgrims are realistic about that. They want to learn from the past and then find new ways to be closer as families and to form community. And they are affirmed by a vision of finding a lifestyle that is in harmony with what Aldo Leopold called THE LAND—"all things on, over and in the earth."

Other pilgrims are discouraged or angry. A man who

quickly identified himself as a Christian, came with a less optimistic view. "Do you know how God is destroying the world this time?" he demanded. "He is doing it with us!"

I tried to tell him there is another side of people. He did not listen, and I wondered what my parents might have said if the man had come to the door of this house in their time. I could imagine Father saying as he so often did, "Well. Things can be changed, you know." My Methodist mother, though, would likely have asked if there was not a contradiction in someone trying to be an Old Testament Christian.

Some pilgrims come with a real life story they want to tell me. They seem certain I will listen but unsure that anyone else will. They make me realize how rarely Americans tell their own stories now that we have allowed entertainment television to speak for us. That is a loss we are paying for. Authentic storytelling helps us know who we are and carries our values to new generations. It celebrates the everyday lives of ordinary people whose stories tell me they are not ordinary at all.

When we stop telling our stories, a Navajo man once told me, we stop being a people.

So the pilgrims and I learn from each other. They help me know that I too am a searching pilgrim, and, like Robert Frost, "I have promises to keep and miles to go before I sleep."

I still have an irresistible urge to push open the door of an old deserted farmhouse to see if those who lived there left fragments of their life story.

I find the sense of human history almost overwhelming in ancient places—the great Toltec and Mayan pyramids of Mexico, the hidden city of Machu Picchu, the pre-Inca ruins of Tiahuanaco on the somber high plateau of Bolivia, the old temples of Sicily and Greece, the austere circles of great stones in the Orkney Islands, off Scotland's northern coast.

I am tempted to say we are all pilgrims in search of something lost or not yet found. Apparently that is not so. I went to England's Stonehenge on a dark day when a cold fall wind was driving low clouds over that empty plain. I came up out of the hidden parking lot, a man and woman with two children following me, the man grumbling, asking how long this was going to take. Suddenly that mysterious circle of stones was before us. I stopped in awe.

The other man stopped and said, "Is that it? Well we don't have to walk all the way round the bloody thing! We can see it from here!" The man herded his family back toward the parking lot, dismissing the 3,500-year-old monument that lay before me.

Stonehenge is a series of circles, the outer earthen one 350 feet across, the tall pillars of the inner circle bridged together at the top by horizontal stones, etching a 22-foot-high silhouette against the sky.

I walked slowly around the inner circle. There were no other visitors. I could hear only my own footsteps and the empty sound of the wind moving through the stones. I did not want to believe the ruins were nothing more than another people's way of asking their own questions. I wanted the place to speak, tell me the hidden *why*.

Far from Stonehenge now, I can laugh at myself a little. I found no answers there. I did not even find the *why* of my questions. Why is there this instinct to search? Why are some of us so drawn to the silent, ancient places?

It is as though, once in childhood, a door opened for a moment and we glimpsed a hint of an obvious answer about who and why we are. But the door closed too quickly, revealing only a promise that an answer does exist.

We must each live with that mystery, compelled either to search or to shutter the mind in denial. As for myself, I have come to realize that I walk near to some ultimate revelation in my closeness to other persons and in my relationship with the land—that entire creation I am part of.

Now, finally, I arrive at the harmony of ideas I have been groping toward. The search of the pilgrims, myself among them, joins with the search that is wrapped in the word "Christmas." They take strength from one another, like the gathering of rivers. It does not matter that the full meaning of the resulting unity is forever just beyond my reach.